Information Technology and Competitive Advantage in Small Firms

Does IT matter? This book argues that even as IT hardware, software, data and associated processes are becoming more of a commodity, it has never been more important to manage IT as a strategic asset. However, managing IT as a strategic asset is notoriously difficult, as is studying the impact of IT on firm performance. This book sets out to identify, explain and critically evaluate current research in this area.

A unique feature of this book is the use of economic theory to explain management theory and its consequences in professional practice. Beginning with a thorough introduction to Schumpeterian economic theory, the authors re-cast the pre-eminent theory in strategic management research (the Resource Based View) in the light of a Schumpeterian analysis and identify Dynamic Capabilities as an extension of, but also a radical departure from, RBV. The role of IT as an endogenous technology is discussed and it is argued that how we define IT determines not only how we study it but also how we use it and benefit from it.

The book is aimed primarily at the academic research market, but should also be of some interest to managers. It is useful more specifically for all those studying business, IT, strategy, management and innovation.

Brian Webb is Senior Lecturer at Queen's University Management School, Belfast, and at the Open University Business School.

Frank Schlemmer is the owner and manager of a number of small independent retail companies based in Germany and holds a doctorate from Queen's University Management School, Belfast.

Routledge Studies in Small Business

Edited by David J. Storey
Centre for Small and Medium Sized Enterprises,
Warwick Business School, UK

Information Technology and Competitive Advantage in Small Firms

Brian Webb and
Frank Schlemmer

Routledge
Taylor & Francis Group

LONDON AND NEW YORK

First published 2008
by Routledge
2 Park Square, Milton Park, Abingdon, Oxfordshire OX14 4RN

Simultaneously published in the USA and Canada
by Routledge
711 Third Avenue, New York, NY 10017

First issued in paperback 2014

Routledge is an imprint of the Taylor & Francis Group, an informa business

© 2008 Brian Webb and Frank Schlemmer

Typeset in Times New Roman by
Rosemount Typing Services, Barjarg Tower, Auldgirth DG2 0TN

British Library Cataloguing in Publication Data
A catalogue record for this book is available from the British Library

Library of Congress Cataloging in Publication Data
Webb, Brian.
  Information technology and competitive advantage in small firms / Brian
  Webb and Frank Schlemmer.
    p. cm.
    Includes bibliographical references and index.
      ISBN 978-0-415-41799-0 (hardcover) – ISBN 978-0-203-89410-1
      (e-book) 1. Information technology–Management. 2. Small
      business–Management. I. Schlemmer, Frank. II. Title.

HC79.I55.W44 2008
004.068–dc22   2008002201

ISBN 978–1–138–86405–4 (pbk)
ISBN 978–0–415–41799–0 (hbk)

Contents

Illustrations

Preface

Alice never could quite make out, in thinking it over afterwards, how it was that they began: all she remembers is, that they were running hand in hand, and the Queen went so fast that it was all she could do to keep up with her: and still the Queen kept crying 'Faster!' but Alice felt she *could not* go faster, though she had no breath to say so. The most curious part of the thing was, that the trees and the other things round them never changed their places at all: however fast they went, they never seemed to pass anything. 'I wonder if all the things move along with us?' thought poor puzzled Alice. And the Queen seemed to guess her thoughts, for she cried, 'Faster! Don't try to talk!'

Not that Alice had any idea of doing *that*. She felt as if she would never be able to talk again, she was getting so out of breath: and still the Queen cried, 'Faster! Faster!' and dragged her along. 'Are we nearly there?' Alice managed to pant out at last.

'Nearly there!' the Queen repeated. 'Why, we passed it ten minutes ago! Faster!' And they ran on for a time in silence, with the wind whistling in Alice's ears, and almost blowing her hair off her head, she fancied.

'Now! Now!' cried the Queen. 'Faster! Faster!' And they went so fast that at last they seemed to skim through the air, hardly touching the ground with their feet, till suddenly, just as Alice was getting quite exhausted, they stopped, and she found herself sitting on the ground, breathless and giddy. The Queen propped her against a tree, and said kindly, 'You may rest a little now.' Alice looked round her in great surprise. 'Why, I do believe we've been under this tree all the time! Everything's just as it was!'

'Of course it is,' said the Queen: 'what would you have it?'

'Well, in *our* country,' said Alice, still panting a little, 'you'd generally get to somewhere else – if you ran very fast for a long time, as we've been doing.'

'A slow sort of country!' said the Queen. 'Now, *here*, you see, it takes all the running you can do, to keep in the same place. If you want to get somewhere else, you must run at least twice as fast as that!'

'I'd rather not try, please!' said Alice. 'I'm quite content to stay here'...

Carroll, Lewis. (1871: 44–47)
Through the Looking-Glass and What Alice Found There

The necessity of 'running fast just to stand still' is familiar to many managers in today's volatile and hyper-competitive business environment, especially when it comes to the strategic management of IT. This book seeks to map out the landscape of action so that managers, unlike Alice, may feel more confident in moving on.

Acknowledgements

The confluence of the strategic management literature, the information technology literature and the small firm literature is wide and fast flowing. This book attempts to bridge this flow using economic and management theory to construct a vantage point from which management researchers and managers may more clearly see the currents that carry them along. In building this construction we are greatly indebted to the sources of our material.

Neither author is an economist. Consequently we are indebted to the authors of a few seminal papers which we used extensively in the writing of this book. These authors may be readily identified by the frequency of their citations. In Chapter 2 we drew heavily upon a selection of analyses of Schumpeterian theory and in particular the work of Warriner (1931); Penrose (1959); Cantwell (2000); Rosenberg (2000); and Prendergast (2006), whom we also thank for commenting on the chapter.

Both authors claim some expertise in the areas of strategic management and information technology but the volume of the literature and the controversy which much of it still generates necessitated also a selective path. In Chapter 3 our analysis of the resource-based view inevitably draws upon the work of Barney (1991) but is sharpened by the critiques and extensions of his work found in Teece *et al.* (1997) and in Eisenhardt and Martin (2000). In Chapter 4 we apply theories and methods found in the literature to our own data and in this we are especially indebted to the work of Powell and Dent-Micallef (1997). Chapter 5 follows a research method developed by Rouse and Daellenbach (1999) and our results are explained using Weick's (1979) theory of enactment.

It goes without saying (but we say it here anyway) that although we acknowledge our debt to these, and indeed all, authors whose work we have used in the writing of this book, the interpretations found in the following pages are all our own, and any errors are entirely our responsibility.

1   Introduction

Setting the scene

Does IT matter? The question was raised most prominently by Carr (2003a; 2004; 2005) who argued that, as information technology's power and ubiquity has grown its strategic importance has diminished. Brown and Hagel (2003) described Carr's (2003a) initial contribution as an 'important, perhaps even seminal, piece'. There is little doubt that Carr's intervention is timely (because there is increasing evidence that IT is becoming a commodity) and provocative (because IT spend continues to take a significant slice of the corporate budget[1]). But is he right?

In his later prediction of 'The end of corporate computing' Carr (2005) cites the development of advanced information technologies such as web services, grid computing and service-oriented architectures as evidence that IT is becoming (or has already become) commoditised. It follows that, because bundles of hardware, software and processes are available to everyone, no one firm can gain a competitive advantage by acquiring and using them. As processes are increasingly bundled with software (for example, a credit checking function has become an automated routine of computer instructions) then opportunities for firms to differentiate on the basis of processes are reduced, and IT (as a bundle of hardware, software and processes) becomes more of a utility.

Carr's questioning of the strategic value of IT has energised academic and practitioner discourse on the relationship between IT and competitive advantage. Unsurprisingly, his thesis has not gone unchallenged. Sward (2006: 7) appears readily dismissive when he writes: 'the response from gurus in the IT field was immediate. Individuals like Paul Strassman, John Seely Brown, and Chris Langdon, along with numerous business school professors, responded, as did several leading CIOs. These individuals outlined counter arguments that were powerful, articulate and persuasive'. However, citing House (2004), he then acknowledges a downside. The responses were targeted at IT professionals, whereas Carr wrote his original article for CEOs. In fact, as we shall discover, there are several good, direct responses to Carr addressed at CEO level and a great deal of intellectual 'heavy lifting' in the strategic management literature that can be used for this purpose.

Brown and Hagel (2003), in one of the rebuttals to which Sward presumably refers, pointed out that 'even though Carr is not [in fact] claiming that IT doesn't matter (rather his main assertion is that IT is diminishing as a source of strategic differentiation)', his message 'is potentially dangerous for it appears to endorse the notion that businesses should manage IT as a commodity input because the opportunities for strategic differentiation with IT have become so scarce'. This, they believe, is a misguided view. On the contrary, 'IT is inherently strategic because of its indirect effects – it creates possibilities and options that did not exist before' and that while 'IT may become ubiquitous [the] insight required to harness its potential will not be so evenly distributed' 2003: 109). Similarly, McAfee (2005) distinguishes between the 'raw materials' of IT (hardware, networks and commercially available software) and the 'finished goods' of IT (technology that can be used productively and that adds value). Although the former are now more available, this does not mean that they can be readily converted into the latter. Smith and Fingar (2003) make a related point when they conclude 'IT doesn't matter – business processes do'.

Brown and Hagel's (2003) response was published two months after Carr's article, and in the same journal (*Harvard Business Review*), under a Letters to the Editor feature. Also included is a much shorter piece by a business school dean that specifically addresses CIOs. More interestingly, the feature includes a reply by Carr (2003b). He thanks both contributors 'for making the valuable point that a company's skill in using its resources, even those that are commodities, is essential to strategic distinctiveness. A superior ability to interpret and act on information has, in particular, always been a hallmark of outstanding companies. That doesn't mean, however, that the systems that provide the information have any intrinsic strategic value. It is not the hammer that makes the carpenter' (2003b: 112). But surely this is the crux of the matter? Here Carr's metaphorical hammer hits the proverbial nail firmly on the head! Can a variable which itself has no intrinsic value (such as IT hardware and software) add value to other variables such that there is a net increase in firm performance and competitive advantage? Carr clearly believes not; others disagree. This book investigates the evidence on both sides of this debate.[2]

Our analysis is based upon an assumption explicit in Schumpeterian economic theory and implicit in much strategic management theory that IT is an endogenous factor of production. Where IT is seen merely as a technology, then it is seen also as an exogenous factor of production, one that has a direct but external impact on firm performance. It also follows that where IT is viewed as an exogenous factor, its introduction will tend to be radical (rather than incremental), its management loosely coupled with other firm resources and capabilities (rather than tightly coupled), and its evaluation in isolation as an independent variable (rather than in conjunction with other co-dependent variables). It is also much more likely to be ineffective. As we shall argue at length in the next chapter, it is through endogenous technological change that firms create real profits, experience real economic growth, and enjoy sustainable competitive advantage. The implications of this argument are profound, shaping not only how we manage IT but how we study it.

The 'productivity paradox' is a case in point. Simply put, the productivity paradox refers to the observation that, although IT expenditure increases, firm productivity stays the same, or actually declines.[3] Carr (2003a: 49) cites two studies which report negative correlation between IT spend and performance. Even Brown and Hagel (2003) accept that there is little evidence of a positive correlation between IT and firm performance.[4] Against this, Brynjolfsson and Hitt (2000) found a positive return on IT investments and Dedrick *et al.,* (2003) concluded that greater investment in IT is associated with greater productivity growth at company and country level. Meanwhile, Rosenberg (2000) argues that it is simply too early to say what the productivity benefits of IT will be because IT itself has changed fundamentally over recent years. To illustrate his point, he makes a comparison with earlier general purpose technologies.

Steam, the railways and electricity burst forth in one relatively concentrated innovation and the opportunity to improve business practices around these technologies was relatively short lived. Further, these technologies achieved standardisation within a relatively short period of time (e.g. railway gauges). IT, on the other hand, is quite different. IT is still expanding and changing at a rapid pace and opportunities to re-design business practices around new technologies remain plentiful. Recent innovations such as web services offer firms the opportunity to crash through several technologies and architectures as they seek to re-engineer their operations, but generally speaking, 'IT's economic impact has come from incremental innovations rather than big bang initiatives' and what has been important has been the 'cumulative effect of sustained changes' (Rosenberg, 2000: 110).

Although IT components are readily and cheaply available, when they are new they are untested in organisational settings and the skills needed to use and manage the technology are in short supply. These are exactly the points made by Brown and Hagel (2003) in their response to Carr. The problem is that these new technologies create so many opportunities, so many tactical and short-term possibilities to improve business practices that organisations frequently fail to see the strategic wood for the operational trees, and opportunities for long-term sustainable advantage are lost. The situation is exacerbated by technology companies whose actions often reinforce the common but misguided belief that IT is an external phenomenon, one best absorbed in manageable chunks of 'big bang' innovations. The recent development and popularisation of web services is one example. More significantly, in the context of a broader discussion of IT and competitive advantage, web services illustrate the evolving relationships between IT (and specifically the internet) and organisational processes, resources and capabilities.

Web services – commodity or capability?

Web services are variously described in the literature as technology (Gottschalk *et al.*, 2002; Lim and Wen, 2003: Joshi *et al.*, 2004), standards (McAfee, 2005), services (Jobber, 1998; Elfatatry and Layzell, 2004) or some combination of these (Hagel and Brown, 2001). The polymorphous nature of web services is reflected in the following definition

> Web services [are] modular internet based business functions that perform specific business tasks to facilitate business interactions within and beyond the organization. By this definition Web services reflect and refer to loosely coupled reusable software components that are able to semantically encapsulate discrete functionality and are programmatically accessible over standard internet protocols.
>
> (Ratnasingam, 2004: 382)

Although sometimes viewed as an extension of electronic data interchange and the internet (Ratnasingam, 2004), web services differ from previous technologies because of the absence of human intervention in key processes (McAfee, 2005). Whereas both EDI and internet technologies rely on human – application and human – human interaction to work (for example, when placing and fulfilling an order on the web) web services require, indeed are predicated upon, no human involvement. That is, a process running on machine A will communicate with a process running on machine B in order to complete a certain task. This task itself will also be a process (for example, performing a customer credit check) and may itself be called by another process. Machine A and machine B, the process which calls them, and the process which in turns calls that process, may be located within the same firm or across two or more different firms.

Whilst it is true that web services are uniquely defined by their ability to enact 'programmatic interaction' (Murtaza and Shah, 2004), nevertheless, 'because web services are essentially described using semi-structured natural language mechanisms, considerable human intervention is needed to find and combine web services into an end application' (Davies *et al.*, 2004). This suggests that individual and organisational capabilities in the development and management of web services will remain important, even as the utility value of the technology declines.

Similar to the internet, because web services are built using open and freely available standards they are relatively inexpensive, simple and quick to develop, certainly in comparison with proprietary based solutions. Rooney (2002) claims that it requires two-thirds less time to build a web service than to develop a typical client/server application. Gillmor (2002) claims a two-thirds cost reduction in a major implementation project when web services were used in preference to a traditional proprietary based approach. Stal (2002) has noted reduced complexity, time and cost and Fletcher and Waterhouse (2002) have noted that users of web services face fewer maintenance costs than those who use competing integration technologies.

Anderson *et al.,* (2005) expanded upon the findings of Dembla *et al.,* (2004) and examined 'the significance of technological, methodological and business factors in contributing to the success of initial web services projects (2005: 66). They used four case studies from the financial services sector. Each case study was evaluated against 36 success factors, derived from the 'industry experiences of several of the authors and a synopsis of practitioner studies' (ibid: 67). Their factors included business client contribution, customer demand and financial rate of return. They ranked business factors ahead of technological factors (which broadly equate to IT knowledge, operations and objects) and methodological factors (which include aspects of dynamic capabilities such as learning, integration and re-configuration). Anderson *et al.,* also found that their (case) 'studies indicate importance in the collateral and incremental benefits of the existing or introduced technological factors in the success of the (web services) projects' (ibid: 73).

The Dembla *et al.* (2004) and the Anderson *et al.* (2005) studies highlight the importance of business factors over technological factors in web services adoption and success. Although their studies were of large firms, we may infer some correspondence in the small firm environment. For example, the first case study in the Anderson *et al.* study was of a smaller and less sophisticated firm than the other three case studies but still ranked business factors ahead of technological and methodological factors (although not so strongly). Better evidence for successful small firm adoption of web services is found when small firms are invited or mandated as suppliers to large firms to join supply chain management systems (Ulfelder, 2003). Murtaza and Shah (2004) suggest that such developments have become a strategic necessity for small firms because 'real time collaboration is a key element of agile manufacturing strategies as it can lead to significant strategic and operational benefits for all business partners' (2004: 50). In high-tech, high-velocity markets, examples of successful implementations are rarer. The way in which small firms collaborated and co-evolved in the creation and development of the ASP[5] industry is one example but even here the industry soon came to be dominated by fewer larger firms, with the result that routines became more established, outcomes more predictable and capabilities less dynamic (Austin, 2002).

A key development in web services (as suggested in Ratnasingam's (2004: 382) definition) is the move to semantic web technology.

> the semantic web will enable the accessing of web resources by semantic content rather than just by keywords. Resources (in this case web services) are defined in such a way that they can be automatically 'understood' and processed by machine. This will enable the realization of semantic web services, involving the automation of service discovery, acquisition, composition and monitoring. Software agents will be able to automatically create new services from already published services, with potentially huge implications for models of eBusiness.
>
> (Davies *et al.*, 2004: 118)

This step change in capability has required a development away from the XML[6] based standards that currently underpin the semantic web (and which underpin web services and internet technologies) to a new language, capable of expressing semantic metadata.[7]

The semantic web promises the emergence of a viable, large-scale utility model based on high-capacity, fibre optic communication networks. If information technology is increasingly seen as a 'general purpose technology' then the semantic web and web services (along with virtualisation and grid computing) represent its transformation into a 'centralized utility' (Carr, 2005).[8] With this model we may suppose that, as the utility value of technology declines, the capability value in building and maintaining web services will increase. With increased 'commoditisation' of IT in the form of web services, superior firm performance will be determined by the ability of the firm to manage IT through a unique set of capabilities (McAfee, 2005).

As more and more service or functional capabilities become embedded in web services software (for example, the capability to perform credit checks or to process payments will be codified in web services software and available across the internet) then firms must compete on other distinct competencies. It is clear that management capabilities will be important to the success of web services implementations; but what sort of capabilities? How will these combine with other strategic assets? And what is the likely impact upon firm performance?

Unfortunately we cannot readily go out and measure such capabilities, particularly in small firms. web services technology is too new, and implementations too few, to make cross-sectional or longitudinal studies feasible. Case studies of web services success stories offer important initial direction, but these cannot substitute for a body of empirical data, and are anyway mostly confined to large firms. In the absence of significant implementations of web services technology, we are left to study 'intermediate' web services adoption, predicated on the internet where 'the web services initiative effectively adds computational objects to the static information of yesterday's web and as such offers distributed services capability over a network' (Davies *et al.*, 2004).

Commonalities between internet adoption and web services adoption may yield important insights into the role of business resources and management capabilities in web services performance. The commonalities go beyond merely technical considerations (where the internet is the 'carrier technology' for web services) to include managerial and organisational considerations (where that same carrier technology facilitates enhanced knowledge management and organisational learning). Whereas the impact of the internet on competency development and organisational learning has already been studied in the small firm environment (for example, Chaston *et al.*, 2001; Pollard, 2003; Martin and Matlay, 2003; Ellis and Wagner, 2005) there is a need to extend this line of inquiry to web services (Webb and Schlemmer, 2008).

Similar to the internet, web services are key enablers of other firm resources and capabilities and are themselves subject to the management of these resources and capabilities. As with the internet, effective knowledge management may depend upon understanding web services as bundles of firm-specific assets that both reflect and contribute towards the management of firm performance in other areas. Indeed (as with the internet), much may be gained from studying the interaction effects or complementarity of web services on other firm resources and capabilities. This suggests that effective knowledge management is best achieved when web services are managed as strategic assets.

Another interpretation of such studies is that they anticipate the commoditisation of technology and capabilities under web services. With the internet/world wide web human–human interactions have been replaced by human–application interactions in the majority of B2B transactions. Web services in turn replace many human–application interactions with program–program or application–application interactions. When a web service is essentially a process that runs on the web, technology and capability are bundled and made freely available. In this scenario competitive advantage will not come from low-level, operational or functional capabilities that are embedded in web services but from higher-level, strategic capabilities that are developed and retained by the firm.[9] This suggests that business and IT resources will be important to building such capabilities and that the mere possession of resources will be insufficient to create competitive advantage from web services (although it may yield some short-term benefits).

We may expect with web services that IT becomes more like a commodity. In fact, the opposite is true. When considered as an asset beyond mere hardware, software and processes, IT has become more strategic because the skills, capabilities and competencies required to build and manage web services successfully are at a premium. Few companies have yet developed these but when they do (and do it well) they are firm-specific, critically path dependent, heterogeneous and inimitable. The related development of service-oriented architecture (SOA) computing is illustrative of this point. A service-oriented architecture, as the name suggests, is the organisational blueprint or framework for web services.[10] It defines and declares all web services, their functionality, availability and use. It determines which web services can be used for which applications, and when and how this may be done. It sets out the relationships between web services and applications, and between web services and other web services. Hence, a service-oriented architecture is something that is built, not bought.

Building a service-oriented architecture, in a company of any size, is a significant undertaking. It is not uncommon for even moderately sized and relatively unsophisticated firms to identify over one thousand services. Because each web service is itself a bundle of hardware, software, data and processes, and the relationship between web services and applications is truly many-to-many,[11] then it is easy to see how the task of building and maintaining a service-oriented architecture can quickly become complex. Of course, web services can and should make corporate computing less complex; software is meant to be designed once, stored in a central repository and called by applications as and when required. However, this presupposes levels of organisational commitment, leadership, discipline, planning, implementation and monitoring that are frequently not found in practice.

The point here is that the technology component of successful web services implementations is relatively unimportant. This technology is ubiquitous, freely available, homogeneous and readily copied. It very closely approximates to a utility service, whether that service is supplied in-house or externally.[12] But the success of web services implementations crucially depends on what is done with that technology. This in turn is determined by the capabilities possessed by the firm. For sure, some of these capabilities are related specifically to the management of technology (technical knowledge, skills and experience, for example) but many are not (for example, general capabilities such as leadership, project management and communication are vitally important to IT success). Even when the adopting firm out-sources much of the IT implementation it still must retain some core capabilities in-house in order to make the implementation work. This is a strategic necessity. To say that IT doesn't matter implies that the management of IT doesn't matter. On the contrary, even as IT has become more of a utility, management of that utility for competitive advantage has become more important.[13]

Anatomy of this text

As Rosenberg (2000) makes clear, IT is not an exogenous but an endogenous factor of production. IT is complex, complementary to other technologies and assets, and incremental. IT evolves primarily not in big bang leaps, but through a quiet succession of incremental steps. As a result, the key to managing IT is not the management of innovation but the management of imitation. Because we view IT wrongly, we measure IT wrongly and reach wrong conclusions about its strategic impact. It may simply be too early to assess the long-term impact of IT because many aspects of that impact are still working themselves out. In this sense, the IT productivity paradox may be more a reflection of our failure to understand the technology than a failure of the technology itself.

We develop these key themes in this text. We examine IT as a dependent and as an independent variable, as a static and a dynamic phenomenon, as a direct (strategic) and indirect (complementary) asset. IT is viewed as an endogenous factor of production and we predict that the ways in which a firm acquires, develops, manages and evaluates IT are different from the ways in which a firm acts where IT is regarded as an exogenous factor. For example, where IT is regarded as an external factor, much more emphasis is placed on acquiring IT and much less emphasis upon integrating IT with other firm-specific resources and capabilities. This puts a premium on certain managerial competencies and behaviours (such as the ability to source and select IT) and de-emphasises others (such as the ability to adapt IT to changing circumstances). It also has a direct impact on firm performance. We reject the IT as commodity argument, in all but narrow interpretations, because it is based upon a fundamental misconception of the nature and role of IT. Exposing this misconception and putting forward an alternative view is a big part of what this book is all about.

The book is structured as follows. In Chapter 2 we review the economic theory upon which much management theory and literature is based. Economics shapes the landscape of action upon which researchers and practitioners operate. Although rarely acknowledged in the management literature, economic theory is at the root of all strategising, the source and the explanation of competitive advantage. Accordingly, we set out some basic economic theory and explain how this impacts upon the work of both researchers and practitioners. For example, we show that how we define competitive advantage determines how we study it, and the outcomes of the study. We show also that competitive advantage is an economic advantage that cannot be achieved by the mere possession of a resource or capability but only by its usage. We introduce the theory of Joseph Schumpeter and examine the theory of IT as an endogenous factor of production. Here the essential logic of our position is first established. IT cannot be a source of Ricardian rents because it does not meet the conditions (of asset heterogeneity and asset immobility) through which Ricardian rents may be generated. However, IT may be a source of Schumpeterian rents because it can enable other strategic assets to meet these conditions, or better to meet these conditions. This chapter provides the foundation for all subsequent chapters. Its logic informs the entire text, structuring the data analysis and conclusions and providing a context for a discussion of their implications.

In Chapter 3 we investigate the out-workings of economic theory in different theories of management. In particular we identify the economic provenance of the resource-based view (RBV) through reference to Schumpeterian economics and Penrose's (1959) application of this theory to the firm. We reject the 'Schumpeterian hypothesis' as a misinterpretation and misrepresentation of the true and radical nature of Schumpeter's theory and instead introduce the theory of dynamic capabilities (Teece *et al.*, 1997; Eisenhardt and Martin, 2000) as the true inheritor of Schumpeterian economics at firm level. The implications of this *denouement* of RBV for the management of IT are explored. The mere possession of IT will not yield competitive advantage but its use, in conjunction with other strategic assets, might. IT requires more than 'mere' management, it requires leadership, entrepreneurship and innovation. We substantiate these deductions in the strategic management literature.

In Chapter 4 we look for evidence that these theories work, in an examination of empirical studies (our own and those of other researchers). We examine the relationship between IT and firm performance by testing theories of direct and contingent effects using research data from the field, including our own study of small firms. We conclude that although there is little support for IT directly impacting firm performance, there is some support for an indirect effect, when IT acts as a complementary resource to other strategic assets. This suggests that IT may not be a source of Ricardian rents but may be a source of Schumpeterian rents.

In Chapter 5 we venture beyond economic theories to explain the development of dynamic capabilities, which we have identified from the literature and from our own research as being vitally important to the building of superior firm performance. We use the theory of enactment (Weick, 1979) to explain the behaviour of owner-managers in small firms as they seek to create competitive advantage. We observe that some owner-managers exhibit a positive enactment between thought and action that drives superior firm performance and some exhibit a negative enactment that drives inferior firm performance. We employ McGregor's seminal dichotomy of X and Y behavioural styles to further explain our observations. We then relate our analysis to broader concepts of IT leadership and innovation. The purpose of this chapter is to show how IT can become a source of Schumpeterian rents.

In Chapter 6 we bring these various strands together to reflect more fully upon the relationship between IT and competitive advantage.

Specifically, we represent this relationship as two managerial paradigms based upon economic and strategic management theory. We label these the classical (Ricardian) and evolutionary (Schumpeterian) approaches. The former is most appropriate during periods of relative equilibrium when 'mere management' is largely sufficient for the daily round, and the latter is most appropriate during periods of disequilibrium when leadership, entrepreneurship and innovation come to the fore. However, we wish to avoid a dichotomy of approaches and emphasise that in practice good managers will adopt both approaches, moving seamlessly between them as circumstances dictate.

The implications of this thinking for technology management are then explored in the context of differences between innovation and imitation. To an increasing extent, empirical studies are suggesting that first movers do not always, or even usually, benefit most from an innovation. Rather, it is imitators who reap the most reward. This suggests that, on occasion, mere management may be more important than leadership and entrepreneurship. It also follows that, because technological imitation is closely linked to absorptive capacity and because a firm's absorptive capacity is crucially dependent upon its resources and capabilities, IT cannot be considered a commodity. We illustrate this point through a discussion of the development of core capabilities and organisational resilience (Prahalad and Hamel, 1990; Hamel and Valikangas, 2003) and by using our own data taken from a study of small IT companies. We conclude that IT does matter, in ways that are often overlooked, sometimes surprising but always worth knowing.

In the remainder of this (current) chapter we wish to establish *a priori* a firm foundation to support our arguments. As we shall presently make clear, in much strategic management research there is often ambivalence and inconsistency in the definition and deployment of the term 'competitive advantage'. Sometimes competitive advantage is defined in purely financial terms, and at other times it is defined in a non-financial way. Sometimes competitive advantage refers to the aggregated level (where it is said that the firm has competitive advantage) and at other times refers to the disaggregated level (where it is said that a sub-unit of the firm or one aspect of the firm's operations has competitive advantage).[14] Even when it is agreed to use quantitative rather than qualitative measures of firm performance there is often disagreement on what those quantitative measures should be. Economic theory provides a clear definition of competitive advantage at firm level but this is difficult to measure in practice. Alternative or surrogate accounting measures are more accessible but are frequently multifarious and multinomial. So our first 'foundation' is a clarification of what we mean by competitive advantage.

Our second foundation is concerned with the nature and role of small firms in competitive strategy. Alhough it is certainly true that small firms are attracting increasing attention from strategic management researchers (as the research agenda has simultaneously shifted from macro to micro investigations of firm differences), the vast majority of the extant strategic management literature is concerned only with large firms. This does not mean that this literature is irrelevant to the study of small firms. However, the researcher of competitive advantage in small firms has a special responsibility to filter and calibrate the literature in a way that is meaningful at this level. Of course, there is much good literature on small firms, and this is increasing in both quantity and quality. Indeed, we claim to make a contribution to this literature through this book.

Competitive advantage and firm performance

Cooper (1993: 251) notes the 'need to understand more fully the effects of different performance measures and whether the factors that enhance performance vary according to the measure used'. A number of studies have shown that the choice and the operationalisation of the performance measures can affect the results and even the conclusions of the research (Kirchoff, 1977; Venkatraman and Ramanujam, 1987; Robinson, 1998). It has been shown that different fields of study use different measures of performance due to differences in their research questions (Hofer, 1983; Venkatraman and Ramanujam, 1986).

An accurate measurement of performance requires a clear definition of the dependent variable but many researchers do not give one (Dess and Robinson, 1984). Porter (2001) asserts that indicators such as stock price, sales, or reduced expenses are necessary but not sufficient indicators of economic value and suggests measuring performance as sustained profitability. Murphy *et al.* (1996) recommend that researchers should explicitly state the specific performance dimension(s) under investigation, provide a theory-based rationale for examining the given dimension(s), and include multiple dimensions of performance where possible.

Although mathematical relationships between different performance measures exist, these measures are rarely interchangeable proxies for each other (Robinson, 1998). Murphy *et al.* (1996) compared different measures of performance commonly used in entrepreneurship research. They found that more than 25 per cent of the measures were *negatively* correlated and therefore the relationship between a given independent variable and a given performance dimension is likely to depend on the particular performance measure used. They remark that 'it is quite possible for an independent variable to be positively related to one performance measure and negatively related to another one' (1996: 21).

The multiple dimensions of firm performance reflect the trade-offs that firms face. Actions taken to improve performance on one dimension may well depress performance on another dimension and have no effect on others (Murphy *et al.,* 1996). A firm investing heavily in IT may be less profitable than another firm not committed to the same level of investment because a substantial portion of its current expenses are used to create future options (Vancil, 1972). Yet, there are clear limits below which a firm's short-term profit performance cannot be allowed to slip in order to survive, which limits its long-term investments. A well-managed firm should be able to steer a middle course, making steady investments of slack resources to generate future options, while replenishing the invested slack resources on a regular basis (Chakravarthy and Lorange, 1984).

There is little consensus on the selection of an appropriate set of measures for assessing firm performance but it is unlikely that any single performance measure could serve the needs of such a diverse set of research questions. Strategy researchers' attention has been drawn repeatedly to the conflicting nature of performance dimensions such as long-term growth and short-term profitability, and the associated problems of combining them into a composite dimension of performance (Venkatraman and Ramanujam, 1986). Schendel and Patton (1978) highlight the need to make differential resource allocations depending on the desired performance outcome, in terms of return on equity (ROE), market share or efficiency. Kirchoff and Kirchoff (1980) provide an empirical illustration of the dilemma of pursuing differential (and sometimes conflicting) strategies to achieve long-term and short-term performance results. Others (for example, Bagozzi and Phillips, 1982; Benson, 1974) advocate a multi-factor model to evaluate performance. Chakravarthy (1986) argues that financial data should be supplemented by data that indicate future performance in order to get a richer understanding of the actual performance of a firm.

Cameron and Whetten (1983) focus on key performance indicators and compare performance with other unbounded constructs such as, for example, intelligence, motivation or leadership. They argue that those concepts are very complex, that it is difficult to define and exactly specify them, and to draw boundaries precisely. They then recommend measuring only limited domains of the performance construct. These measures can be accounting-based, financial-market based or non-financial. The evaluation of performance in terms of financial performance has been the dominant concept in strategic management research (Hofer, 1983). Typical accounting-based variables are sales, sales growth and profitability, and for publicly held companies accounting measures are usually available as secondary sources.

However, performance measures rooted in financial accounting have been criticised (Chakravarthy, 1986) because of the scope for accounting manipulation, under-valuation of strategic assets, distortions due to depreciation policies, inventory valuation and treatment of certain revenue and expenditure items, differences in the methods of consolidating accounts, and differences due to lack of standardisation in international accounting conventions. In addition, accounting measures record only past performance and historical trends. Monitoring a firm's strategy requires measures that can also capture its potential for performance in the future and the market value of firms is frequently used as one such measure. Share prices are supposed to reflect the value of firms because they are assumed to reflect the discounted value of all future cash flows and incorporate all relevant information. However, especially for e-commerce companies, signals from the stock market have been unreliable because future profits have been unpredictable (Porter, 2001). Further, the market price would reflect the real value of the firm only if all relevant information were available to market traders, which – as an approximation to a perfectly competitive market – is very unlikely (McWilliams and Siegel, 1997).

A broader conceptualisation of firm performance encompasses non-accounting metrics including market share, new product introduction and competitive position. The inclusion of strategic performance indicators takes us beyond the 'black box' approach that seems to characterise the exclusive use of financial indicators to factors that might lead to financial performance (Venkatraman and Ramanujam, 1986). This shift in research focus from lagging to leading indicators of performance reflects concerns at firm level, where competition is increasingly intense and volatile (as in virtual markets).

A summary of the strengths and weaknesses of the different dimensions of performance measures is given in Table 1.1. Following Cameron and Whetten (1983), three performance dimensions suggest three types of measurement: accounting-based measures, financial market measures and non-financial measures.

Financial performance is a common and an extremely important dependent variable in strategic management. However, the examination

Table 1.1 Dimensions of performance

	Accounting-based measures	Financial market measures	Non-financial measures
Strengths	• 'Hard data' • Often easily available	• Future oriented	• Future oriented
Weaknesses	• Accounting manipulation • Limited to historical trends • Varying accounting conventions • Exclude intangible assets	• Distorted market signals • Market traders may not be completely informed	• Relationship to financial performance may be ambiguous • Managers' perceptions can be biased

of more disaggregated levels of performance in addition to financial performance yields a number of advantages (Ray *et al.*, 2004). Companies may have competitive advantages in some areas and competitive disadvantages in others. For example, competitive advantages that are created by using IT can be neutralised by other disadvantages or appropriated by various stakeholders before they increase financial performance. A firm may excel in some business processes, be average in others, and be bad in still other ones. Financial performance depends, among other things, on the net effect of its processes. Deploying IT performance, as a disaggregated dependent variable instead of, or in addition to, financial performance can facilitate the testing of resource-based logic (Ray *et al.*, 2004) by enabling a comparison of the relationship between strategic assets and financial performance with the relationship between strategic assets and IT performance.

In this book we follow Foss (2005) in arguing that above average, superior or abnormal profits (defined as economic rents) are a valid measure of competitive advantage. It follows then that the relationship between firm performance (measured as the creation of economic rents) and competitive advantage is symbiotic. When we measure one, we measure the other, and for all practicable purposes the two concepts are interchangeable. This position is both simple and elegant. There is no question of the direction or causality of the relationship. It is not necessary to argue that superior firm performance leads to competitive advantage or, alternatively, that competitive advantage leads to superior firm performance. Thus we avoid a common pitfall for many strategic management researchers.

We acknowledge that this stance is not without criticism. Newbert (2007: 141) contends that a firm can create and sustain a competitive advantage (in resources and capabilities) but still not enjoy superior firm performance because the advantage obtained may be appropriated before it is reflected in firm performance. This is commonly said of IT, and indeed, one of our goals in measuring internet performance as well as financial performance (in Chapter 4, and in Schlemmer and Webb, 2006) is to measure the effective use of resources and capabilities at the disaggregated (sub financial) level. We also agree (in Chapters 3 and 4) that measuring disaggregated levels of performance facilitates the testing of resource-based theory. However, we do not advocate disaggregated measures of performance as an alternative to aggregated measures but rather view these as complementary.[15]

Implicit in Newbert's position are two points of departure with our analysis. First, competitive advantage is an independent variable rather than a dependent variable, and second, the relationship between competitive advantage and firm performance is unidirectional, that is, while competitive advantage can lead to increased firm performance, increased firm performance cannot lead to competitive advantage. On the latter point, Newbert quotes Powell (2001) who argues that by treating firm performance and competitive advantage interchangeably, scholars were accepting the tenuous assumption that because a firm has achieved above normal performance it must have, by default, obtained a competitive advantage. Powell argues that tests relying on evidence of the latter as proof of the former are methodologically flawed.

But, we ask, what is the alternative? If competitive advantage is not measured as superior or abnormal firm performance (or economic rents) how then is it to be measured? What assessment of resources and capabilities would be deemed to offer firm competitive advantage? How do we know, for example, in the absence of agreed terms, conditions and measures, whether the performance of company A is better than the performance of company B? How do we assess a single company's performance over time in a way that can be compared with other firms, and the industry average? Obviously many measures of firm performance other than financial performance exist, but how, when and where do these signify competitive advantage? More importantly, if a firm does not enjoy superior firm performance, how relevant can any competitive advantage be?

In Chapter 4 we introduce a study of performance-leading and performance-lagging firms in order to assess the impact of IT as a complementary asset. We determined which firms were leading and which firms were lagging by measuring their financial performance (as

Powell and Dent-Micallef (1997) and many other researchers have done). This is a simple and elegant expedient. The alternative was to determine IT leading and IT lagging firms using some other measure or measures of IT capability. But such measures have proved to be difficult and unreliable in the past. How do we measure IT capability? What measure or measures do we take? And how do we compare these with other companies?

An additional problem is the 'halo effect' (Brown and Perry, 1994). This occurs when the selection of a firm ostensibly on the basis of (say) its IT capability is unduly influenced by prior knowledge of the firm's financial performance. So, successful high-performance companies are selected as IT leaders even though there is little evidence to support a link between IT capability and firm performance. Bharadwaj (2000) calculated a 'halo index' for IT leading firms based upon prior financial performance in an effort to discount undue influence in the selection of firms but did not find sufficient statistical evidence to support this. The problem is that when IT performance is not measured in relation to financial performance, how then is that firm's IT capability to be measured?

In 1995 (as reported by Santhanam and Hartono in 2003) *Information Week* gave up trying to avoid the halo effect and simply ranked IT leaders according to the firm's overall financial performance. It would seem that this is the expedient that most researchers should follow until such time as an IT capability index can be validated. Santhanam and Hortono (2003) call for the development of such a set of measures but do not say what it might be, or even enunciate its features. The approach taken in this book may be considered a (modest) contribution to this research because we evaluate the impact IT assets (comprising resources and capabilities) have on firm performance.

Competitive advantage and small firms

Early strategic management research highlighted the strategic advantages of the high market shares enjoyed by large firms. The PIMS database[16] (for example Gale, 1972) supported the belief that growth strategies to capture market power, scale and other benefits were a 'magic bullet' for creating competitive advantage. However, by the late 1970s researchers realised that small firms have certain competitive advantages over their larger competitors and that low market share did not automatically cause poor performance (Hameresh *et al.*, 1978; Woo and Cooper, 1981). Similarly, Porter (1980; 1985) suggested that niche or focus strategies can be a source of competitive advantage. These findings challenged the basic assumptions of the relationship between market share and competitive advantage. Subsequently, new research streams, such as entrepreneurship and new ventures, developed to examine the role of venture strategy, industry structure and competitive dynamics (Carter *et al.,* 1994; Covin and Slevin, 1990; Dean and Meyer, 1996; McDougall *et al.,* 1994; Sandberg and Hofer, 1987).

One stream of research compared the structures and behaviours of SMEs[17] with their larger competitors. For example, SMEs have a simpler organisational structure than larger enterprises and (subsequently) they experience less structural inertia (Hannan and Freeman, 1984). Small firms perform some activities with less expertise because they do not have functional specialists (Verhees and Meulenberg, 2004). They are often governed by owner-managers, and the vast majority of strategic decisions are usually made by one person (Schlenker and Crocker 2003; Feindt *et al.,* 2002) who often has a reactive and fire-fighting mentality (Hudson *et al.,* 2001) and an entrepreneurial orientated and risk seeking leadership style (Hitt *et al.,* 1991; Woo, 1987).

Jones (2004) shows that in small companies the owner-managers' 'habits of thoughts' strongly affect organisational performance. A manager could be either curious or indifferent about learning and change. These 'habits of thoughts' determine a manager's attention to the firm's routines that support a firm's learning capabilities. Sub-optimal learning processes restrict the firm's growth potential. In Chapter 5 we examine the role of the owner-manager in the creation of dynamic capabilities in small firms. In Chapter 6 we reflect upon this research in a discussion of core competences and the development of the organisational resilience.

Another stream of research examines how small firms differ in their strategic assets from large companies. It has been suggested that small firms frequently suffer from 'resource poverty' (Welsh and White, 1981) which adversely affects strategy development and creates perceptual and physical barriers to growth (Fillis *et al.,* 2004). For example, small companies usually have fewer financial and human resources (Chow *et al.,* 1997; Caldeira and Ward 2003; Ihlstrom and Nilsson, 2003; Gribbins and King, 2004); are usually not able to achieve cost leadership (Porter, 1980; Lee *et al.,* 1999); often have problems bringing innovations to market (Abernathy and Utterback, 1978) and face problems of legitimacy (Chen and Hambrick, 1995) because larger firms are better known and have a better reputation which can be a source of competitive advantage (Fombrun and Shanley, 1990).

However, small firms are adept at pursuing strategies built upon the strengths of speed, niche-filling capabilities and flexibility (Dean *et al.*, 1998) and can challenge competitors more actively and act faster than large companies. Chen and Hambrick (1995) found that small firms were more active in initiating competitive moves, but that their speed in executing actions was often countered by large firms' speed in announcing responses. They found that small firms more actively initiated competitive challenges and were speedy but low-key, even secretive, in executing their actions. Yet, small firms were less likely to respond to aggressive actions of their competitors than larger firms. Furthermore, small companies were often very effective in focusing their strategic moves and innovation in a narrow domain (Hameresh *et al.*, 1978).

Smith *et al.* (2001) report that larger firms are better able to influence their environment and buffer themselves against competitors and therefore better able to carry out more effective and timely competitive actions. Large firms are more likely to carry out more total competitive moves in a given time period (Young *et al.*, 1996) and to carry out actions that are strategic in nature and are visible (Chen and Hambrick, 1995). Miller and Chen (1994; 1996) found that large firms are less prone to competitive inertia (measured as the number of responses) and are more likely to employ a single competitive repertoire (i.e. the firm's set of competitive actions consisted of only a few different types). Whereas large firms were found to conceive more quickly of and announce responses to their rival's actions, they were slower than small firms in terms of the time that elapsed between the announcement of their response and its actual implementation (Chen and Hambrick, 1995).

Organisational age (which is highly correlated with organisational size in competitive dynamic research studies) is another indication of the differences between large firms' and small firms' competitive actions. As organisations get older they tend to repeat strategies that have proved successful in the past (Lant *et al.*, 1992; Miller and Chen, 1996). Therefore they tend to become less aware of the competitive environment and more predictable. Younger firms are more dynamic precisely because they do not have access to this organisation and industry experience (Miller and Chen, 1996; Singh *et al.*, 1986). However, younger firms are at a disadvantage because it takes time to gain such experience and they face a struggle to obtain the resources (including institutional recognition) from older firms and customers.

Thong (2001) developed a resource-based model to analyse resource constraints and information systems (IS) implementation in Singaporean small businesses and found that access to external technical expertise is an important factor of IS implementation success. Duhan *et al.* (2001) analysed the role of property-based and knowledge-based resources for IS strategies of a not-for-profit organisation. In particular, they discussed the role of IS as firm resources in SMEs. They focused on strategic IS planning and suggested that it can be enhanced by operations management, marketing support and the firm's knowledge base. Caldeira and Ward (2003) deployed the RBV to explain success with the adoption and use of information systems in manufacturing SMEs. Their in-depth case studies on 12 SMEs suggest that management perspectives and attitudes towards IT adoption and use, and the development of internal IT competence are success factors for the usage of IT.

Internet researchers have also studied SMEs. One finding is that when SMEs deploy internet technology they are usually more entrepreneurial and willing to experiment and innovate with business models than their larger competitors with established hierarchies. On the other hand, small companies are restricted by their limited resources (Jutla *et al.,* 2002). The resource poverty of SMEs limits their marketing options using the internet compared with larger companies (Jones, 2004). Saban and Rau (2005) found that resource and knowledge limitations hamper the usage of websites by SMEs. It has also been suggested that SMEs use the internet less strategically (Webb and Sayer, 1998) and less for marketing purposes (BarNir *et al.*, 2003) than their larger competitors.

In this book we claim a contribution to the literature on small firms and competitive strategy in general, and on e-business small firms and competitive strategy in particular through the inclusion of our own research into SMEs. Although aspects of this research have been published previously (for example, see Schlemmer and Webb, 2006), we include here for the first time an analysis of an expanded data set specifically designed to compare and contrast the direct and indirect impact of IT and the internet on small firm financial performance. In addition to the dearth of literature on small firms and competitive strategy already noted, there is an under-representation of studies into the role and impact of IT in such environments. Most noticeably, there is a shortage of empirical studies into the indirect impact of IT on firm performance in its role as a complementary asset. These gaps are addressed predominantly in Chapters 4 using quantitative research methods but also in Chapter 5 when we discuss the development of dynamic capabilities using qualitative research methods.

A note on theory and practice

A sub-title of this book might be 'theory and practice'. This is certainly its subtext. In the reference disciplines of strategic management and IS, almost every major journal and conference over the past few years has included some discussion of the relationship between theory and practice and many textbooks explicitly address the issue. Even a cursory reading of the strategic management literature shows that the relationship between theory and practice is an issue of real concern to researchers, and of real consequence to practitioners. Understanding and explaining this relationship has become essential to rigour and relevance in the field. The discipline of IS illustrates this point well. Here the gap between theory and practice appears to be widening. On the one hand, there appear to be an increasing number of high-profile IS project failures, and on the other hand, an increasing number of theories which attempt (but generally fail) to explain these failures.[18] Meanwhile the (often sterile) debate over the IT productivity paradox continues. Managers may be forgiven for feeling confused and frustrated.

When IT is treated as an exogenous factor of production, as it frequently is by researchers and practitioners alike, we should not be surprised that firms find it difficult to integrate IT with other firm resources and capabilities, and to account for their successes and failures. However, when IT is viewed as an endogenous technology, something developed within and of the firm, its integration with other strategic resources becomes feasible, if never easy, and the prospects for firms using IT for competitive advantage improve, even as it remains difficult to quantify such improvements. Thus technological endogeneity is a core theory underpinning this book. This is based upon Schumpeterian economic theory, Penrose's (1959) application of this theory to the firm, and the evolutionary theory of technological change (Nelson and Winter, 1982; Rosenberg, 1982).

Yet it is important to point out at the outset that although this book is intimately concerned with theory, and the application of theory in practice, this concern does not extend to the development of prescriptive frameworks, models or methods that purport to make the transition from theory to practice (and from practice to theory) better. We recognise that this is a legitimate and important research area (for example, Curley, 2004 and Sward, 2006 have developed methods for evaluating the business benefits of IT) but it is not the concern of this book. Nevertheless in the concluding chapter (Chapter 6) we suggest ways in which our work might contribute to such outcomes.

2   IT and economic theory

Introduction

In this chapter we examine the relationship between IT and competitive advantage from the perspective of economic theory. We first examine the nature of competitive advantage which we define as economic rents, a concept that has strong theoretical validity but weak empirical reliability in the strategic management literature. We examine the creation of economic rents in two distinct but overlapping realms of economic activity – equilibrium and disequilibrium. We focus on disequilibrium as a source for innovation and long-term economic growth. We examine the concept of complementarity, the value of IT as a general purpose technology and the importance of imitation as well as innovation in realising long-term benefits from technology. Taking the concept of equilibrium as a point of departure between classical and evolutionary economic theories, we examine the major components of Schumpeterian theory to better explain the role of technology. These are Schumpeter's vision, and his views on innovation, leadership, entrepreneurship and management. Our intention is to link the practice of management to economic theory in a way that is transparent (the actions of managers are clearly grounded in the economic system in which they operate) and relevant (economic theory is 'the elephant in the room' which sets the parameters for management strategy).

Economic rents as competitive advantage

Pareto (1848–1923) defined rent as 'a payment to a factor over and above what is necessary to keep it in its present employment'. Any factor (land, labour or capital) which is insufficiently rewarded in its present occupation will move to seek out a better reward elsewhere. To keep a factor employed in its current occupation it must earn (or be rewarded with) an amount at least equal to its 'transfer earnings'. Transfer earnings are the amount the factor would earn in its best paid alternative employment. This amount is also known as the factor's 'opportunity cost'. So economic rent is the payment to a factor over and above what is necessary to keep that factor in its current employment (that is, a payment to a factor less its opportunity or transfer cost). This definition of economic rents illustrates two important aspects about the study of competitive advantage. First, the definition of competitive advantage determines what is measured and the outcomes of the study. Second, it determines the difference between accounting measures of profit and economic measures of profit.

For accountants, 'profit' is the difference between the sale price of a good or service and its cost of production. But economists include also the opportunity cost, or the cost of alternative uses of the factors used to produce that profit. Critically, economists make a distinction between 'normal profit' and 'economic rent'. Normal profit is defined as an acceptable or reasonable return on the capital invested in producing that profit. This is the minimum return necessary to continue production, since if a factor of production is not producing a return at least equivalent to what could be earned in alternative employment, then that capital will move elsewhere in pursuit of higher returns. In a perfect market, the free flow of capital will mean that all firms achieve normal profits, and there will be no economic rents, which are defined as a return above normal profits, sometimes also known as super-profits. And without economic rents no firm can have a competitive advantage.

However, markets are not perfect in real life. There will be some aspect of industry structure (such as unequal access to raw materials) or firm performance (such as the quality of the workforce outputs) that creates distortions in the market. It is these distortions or differentials in the market that make abnormal profits or economic rents possible. Economists further distinguish between *quasi*-rents and *monopoly* rents.

Quasi-rent is a term originally coined to distinguish between rent earned from land and rent earned by capital and labour.[1] Today, the term quasi-rent is often used to refer to *temporary* rents – rents which will eventually be eliminated by competition. Common examples include abnormal rents derived from shortages of capital, shortages of labour or shortages of land. Quasi-rents may also be achieved by a shortage of competition (being first to market) or by a shortage of know-how (which is really a shortage of labour, where differences result from different levels of ability in the workplace, known also as 'rent of ability').

Monopoly rent is achieved by successfully excluding competitors from the industry *over the longer term* (to distinguish this type of abnormal rent from quasi- or temporary rents). Sources of monopoly rents include patents, copyrights, branding and market power. The point is that, even with so-called monopoly rents, any competitive advantage (through the achievement of abnormal or economic rents) will sooner or later be removed. Patents and copyrights expire, branding is eroded by competition, and market power is diminished.

Economic theory suggests that sustainable competitive advantage cannot come from the mere possession of a factor, but may come from the use of the factor (usually in combination with other factors). Possession of a factor may produce short-term or temporary competitive advantage. For example, economic rent from land (the difference between the current value of the land and the value of its alternative use, and therefore not to be confused with commercial rent) may be obtained where there is a distortion in the market and prices are fixed or artificially high due to demand outstripping supply. The owner of commercial property will enjoy economic rents where there is limited supply of commercial premises but strong demand. When the distortion of the market is eased or removed – in this case by the opening up of nearby adjacent property of similar standard – this competitive advantage will be reduced or eliminated.

The factory owner who installs new plant and machinery will not achieve sustainable competitive advantage simply by buying and owning this machinery. Rather, sustained competitive advantage can come only from the use of this machinery, for example in cutting materials more precisely, with less waste, such that the factory becomes more efficient and therefore more profitable. Neither should we expect the mere ownership of IT to produce competitive advantage. Increased efficiencies in productive processes gained from factory or office automation will be short lived because freely available IT may be implemented in a similar or better way by the competition. If many (or all) firms enjoy the same efficiency gains through IT then none can be said to have a competitive advantage. However, it also follows that where IT is *not* freely available (because IT is an endogenous strategic asset, bound up with or bundled with other strategic assets specific to the firm) then it may be a source of sustainable competitive advantage.

The important observation that IT alone will not create competitive advantage, if somewhat obvious from an economist's point of view, has been belatedly accepted within the IS community, as empirical studies increasingly failed to report a positive correlation between IT spend and firm financial performance (see Wade and Hulland, 2004 for a review). Following the 'golden era' of strategic Information Systems (*circa* 1975–1990) based upon a few famous case studies including American

Airlines Sabre, McKesson's Economist, and Merrill Lynch's joined-up banking, initial optimism gave way to a realism that IT was not a source of competitive advantage but rather a competitive necessity. Unfortunately, as we shall see from our discussion of the strategic management literature in the next chapter, this new pragmatism has been slow to establish itself as accepted theory and practice.

Foss (2005) has advocated the use of economic rents as a dependent variable in strategic management research because the term is 'unambiguously defined and consistently used in the literature'. Yet, the term is still not widely used as an operational measure of firm performance because there is no consensus on how economic rents should be measured. Rather, despite some acknowledgement of the elegance and utility of the term from a theoretical perspective, researchers tend to use surrogate accounting measurements. These include, but are by no means limited to, return on investment (ROI), return on equity (ROE), and economic value added (EVA). These performance measures vary widely.[2]

Where the use of accounting performance measures correlates highly with economic rents, it may be argued, from a statistical point of view at least, that the measures are interchangeable. We do not deny that practical problems exist in the use of economic rents as a dependent variable of firm performance in strategic management research. We readily acknowledge that whereas economic rents are a powerful underlying concept, researchers often use proxy (and frequently accounting) measures of performance. Indeed, that is what we have done in our own research. This caveat reduces any discussion of economic rents to two valuable insights. First, the concept (and application) of economic rents is an important reminder of the limitations of firm competitive advantage. Second, it suggests that a fruitful area for research is into the usage, rather than the mere ownership, of resources.

Equilibrium and disequilibrium

In economics, the concept of equilibrium is central to different explanations (or theories) of the economy, and to differences between these.[3] The concept of equilibrium itself is simple (and therein lies its explanatory power), but its interpretation in theories of economic systems, which include a full account of its causes and consequences, is often complex.

In perfectly competitive markets (also known as PCE),[4] price adjusts upwards or downwards to achieve a balance, or equilibrium, between the goods coming in for sale and those requested by purchasers. That is, demand and supply react on one another until a position of stable equilibrium is reached where the quantities of goods demanded exactly equal the quantities supplied (and the market is cleared). This equilibrium is disturbed by changes in the demand and supply of goods – demand may increase or decrease, supply may increase or decrease. Because the market price does not adjust instantly, opportunities are created for firms to take advantage of the discrepancy between supply and demand and the time-lag in price adjustment to achieve excess or surplus profits. So, for example, where demand for a particular good or service outstrips supply, a firm that is in a position to supply into that market will benefit from increased prices. But this advantage is necessarily only temporary. As prices rise, other suppliers will be attracted into the market, supply will increase to meet demand, and prices will fall. The disturbance is short-term, as eventually the market will adjust itself and price equilibrium will be restored. Thus, in perfectly competitive markets, the economic system is self-regulating and essentially static.[5]

This economic system (of perfect competition) determines the nature and role of individual firms within it. At industry level the demand curve is downward sloping (as price increases, demand decreases), but for the individual firm the demand curve is horizontal, because (by definition), in perfect competition no one firm is large enough to influence price in the market. What one firm brings to the market will immediately be purchased at market price. However, in real life, perfect market competition rarely exists, it is disrupted by distortions and inefficiencies in the supply and demand of goods and services, and individual firms can take advantage of this.

In Ricardian, classical, and neo classical economic theory, rent is appropriated by one firm or a few firms based on exploitation of imperfections or inefficiencies in the market, or disturbances in the price system, to gain competitive advantage using market power. Temporary monopolies result from differences in firm resources because some firms will have (or will have access to) expertise in the use of specific resources that other do not. The market is stationary or growing at a steady state within an established market structure. Growth results from 'a simple reproduction of at least some existing elements of the economy on an expanded scale' (Cantwell, 2000: 6). An increase in profits is due to an increase in market power. So growth is market driven, incremental, and largely predictable and rent is a return to a position of market power.

At disequilibrium, on the other hand, growth is inherently revolutionary rather than evolutionary. Schumpeter (1942)[6] referred to this as 'creative destruction'. Cantwell and Fai (1999) point out that this term is often misunderstood since the disruption refers to the circular flow and established market structures but the creative process itself is likely to be cumulative and incremental. One consequence of this misinterpretation is that the impact of the creative process *per se* is often overestimated, when it is the combination of (incremental) creativity and disruptive market change that is really important. An over emphasis on the initial act of innovation at the expense of subsequent developments of that innovation through imitations, is – as we shall see in the next chapter – prevalent in much of the strategic management literature.

In Schumpeterian economics, rents are a return to the firm for bearing the uncertainty inherent in innovation during periods of disequilibrium. Under Ricardian equilibrium, risk can be estimated and to some extent planned for, that is, it can be insured against (Mathews, 2006: 101). Therefore, as part of the factor, it cannot be a part of the residual (or profit). In Schumpeterian disequilibrium, uncertainty can lead to profit (as a residual category of income), because it cannot (by definition) be predicted or planned. Profit is a reward to the bearer of uncertainty, who is the entrepreneur. During periods of equilibrium, risk can be a source of short-term advantage (through market position) but cannot be a source of long-term advantage.

According to Schumpeterian economic theory, profits are more evenly spread and socially beneficial because they are the result of creative processes that add to the income stream, and not the result of the exercise of market power that exploits existing flows within the income stream. Market power may indeed result from innovation, even during periods of creative disruption, and this power may increase profits, but this is a co-incidental by-product of this process, caused by the uneven character of the creative process and will eventually be whittled away through competition.

Market power is not an end in itself but a means to an end – it offers the holder some protection and space for long-range planning. Thus the creation of monopoly position through innovation can facilitate learning and knowledge transfer and provide some stability in a volatile environment in order to increase profits (Cantwell, 2000: 10) so that 'the main value to a concern of a single seller position that is secured by patent or monopolistic strategy does not consist so much in the opportunity to behave temporarily according to the monopolistic schema, as in the protection it affords against temporary disorganisation of the market and the space it secures for long range planning' (Schumpeter, 1943: 102–103).

Cantwell (2000: 10) argues that this quotation refutes the 'Schumpeterian hypothesis' because 'it challenges the very notion of analysing innovation as the outcome of the degree of market power associated with one particular kind of market structure as opposed to another'. As we shall discuss later, the 'Schumpeterian hypothesis' is in fact a misinterpretation and misrepresentation of Schumpeterian economic theory found to underpin much strategic management theory.

Circular flow

The theory of circular flow refers to the flow of money around the economy in the form of earnings (rent, wages, profits and interest) or expenditure (consumption). The flow is from entrepreneurs (as earnings) to the general public (as consumption). When all earnings received by the general public are returned to entrepreneurs, we say the economy is in equilibrium. It is static, neither growing nor contracting. In practice this is unlikely because some people (most likely the better-off who have a higher propensity to save) will defer some consumption and save instead, investing in a bank or other financial institution. The banks will in turn lend on these savings (as multiples) to entrepreneurs who will use the money to invest in new plant or machinery, and thus expand their output, and the economy grows. If, however, earnings drop (for example, due to lack of investment) or consumption falls, or both, then the economy contracts. It was a sustained period of the latter scenario in the 1930s that led Keynes (1936) to advocate government intervention to get the economy moving again.

At this stage it is important to point out that, whether the economy is static, growing, or contracting, the underlying economic model is unquestioned. That is, whereas economists disagreed about how the model worked, or on how to get it to work better, the fundamental concepts of demand and supply, and equilibrium tendencies in prices, wages and income were not challenged (not even by Marx, who was primarily concerned with the distribution of wealth and not with its creation). So, although Keynes was radical in his advocacy of government intervention to stimulate demand (in contrast to the *laissez-faire* approach of Smith and Ricardo), he did not question the underlying logic of the economic model. Rather, he was concerned to develop and refine the model to alleviate the worst conditions of the great depression. His recommendations were intended to return the model to an appropriate level of equilibrium, wherein the circular flow of income was sufficient to meet the basic needs of all the population.[7]

Neither did Schumpeter reject the concept of equilibrium (indeed, as we shall see, he was an admirer of Walrasian equilibrium) but like Keynes he was concerned to address the problems of what happened when equilibrium broke down, or otherwise functioned in an unsatisfactory manner. Unlike Keynes, who concentrated on the demand side, Schumpeter concentrated on the supply side. In this respect Schumpeter returned to basics, and focused (as Adam Smith had done) on the activities of the entrepreneur. It was the entrepreneur acting on the supply side, and not the government acting on the demand side, that must drive the economy. It was the entrepreneur – through leadership and innovation – that created new wealth that added to the circular flow of income.[8]

Nowadays governments tend to deploy a mixture of supply-side measures in attempting to manage the economy, including monetarist and fiscal policies but also specific policies to encourage enterprise. These interventions are designed to maintain a steady state, to return to a steady state after a period of disruption, and to grow the economy. So, far from being an alternative to classical or neo-classical economics, Schumpeterian economics can, in this sense, be seen as an extension of it – and its popularisation as 'evolutionary economics' entirely appropriate. This is not to deny the radical nature of Schumpeter's theories but to acknowledge that these co-exist alongside more traditional approaches which are equally valid in their own terms. The lesson for management researchers is that both classical economics and Schumpeterian economics are important in explaining different aspects of strategy, and the success of its implementation.

Schumpeter's analysis

Schumpeter addressed the limitations of static equilibrium theory head-on. Rather than tinker with the existing theory to make it more responsive and dynamic, he proposed an entirely new method of analysis. In time, this became known as evolutionary economics.[9] But Schumpeter clearly admired static equilibrium theory as a logical construct. He praised Walras, saying 'the theory of general equilibrium is Walras' claim to immortality, that great theory whose crystal-clear train of thought has illuminated the structure of purely economic relationships with the light of one fundamental principle' and 'his system of economic equilibrium, uniting as it does, the quality of "revolutionary" creativeness with the quality of classic synthesis, is the only work by an economist that will stand comparison with the achievements of theoretical physics' (Schumpeter and Schumpeter

1954: 827) Yet Schumpeter believed that static equilibrium never was, and never could be, a reality.[10]

Warriner (1931: 40) raises the important question of exactly where this left Schumpeter's analysis. Does static equilibrium work despite the restraints which are placed on it, or is static equilibrium itself a constraint? Warriner observes that Schumpeter resolves this dilemma by re-defining static equilibrium as a dynamic system. 'Schumpeter places it by holding that the law works in any economic system, so far and only so far as economic subjects adapt themselves to changes. To that extent the whole system is static, though not necessarily stationary; it changes but does not itself generate any change. It may grow, by increase of population or expansion of the area of cultivation, but it adapts itself to, and does not develop itself from, the given conditions' (Warriner, 1931: 41).

Schumpeter identified a key weakness in the theory of static equilibrium: because the theory is underpinned by value theory, it cannot explain economic surpluses, since all earnings are consumed. Yet surpluses are a fact of life and their presence must be explained by something. Their presence suggests some sort of change but a static system in its (theoretical) natural state does not generate change, and to admit that change was caused by exogenous factors was to resort to giving a non-economic answer to an economic question. Schumpeter solved this dilemma by introducing change into the static system. Surpluses are the result of the acquisitive motive (*Erwerbsprinzip*) which he treats as a special kind of economic activity and 'on to this concept of economic activity he throws the whole weight of his theory of economic development' (Warriner, 1931: 42). This activity may be described as *innovation* meaning any interference in the adapting system, or interstitial adjustment.

It is important to note that even endogenous change produces only temporary monopoly rents. Any innovation that is introduced is (sooner or later) imitated and surpluses accruing to one or a few firms are competed away. Also, because innovation itself is part of a self-replicating economic activity, although it may cause disruption in the short term, in the long term it will occasion a return to equilibrium. That is, innovation will increase production and earnings but also increase consumption since every new combination requires new productive factors and therefore generates new purchasing power. However, although surpluses from individual innovations are eventually competed away and must eventually occasion a return to equilibrium, continuing cycles or waves of innovation (happening within and between firms and sometimes barely noticeable on the outside) combine to create sufficient surpluses to grow the economy.

Schumpeter did not reject the concept (or theoretical value) of static equilibrium, but believed that it needed to be adapted to account for real economic forces. His solution was to introduce a dynamic element in the form of endogenous change, a special economic activity, which he characterised as innovation. Rather than reject static equilibrium, Schumpeter augmented it with a new system that accounted for disequilibrium and both systems were necessary to the development of his economic theory. His intention is clearly set out in one of his early papers:

> to relegate to one distinct body of doctrines the concept, the continuous curves and small marginal variations, all of which in their turn link up with the circular flow of economic routine under constant data, and to build up alongside of this, and before taking account of the full complexity of the real phenomena, secondary waves, chance occurrences, 'growth' and so on, a theory of capitalistic change, assuming in doing so that non-economic data are constant and gradual change in economic conditions is absent.
>
> (Schumpeter, 1928; quoted in Warriner, 1931: 46)

Warriner argues that in simultaneously criticising static equilibrium while holding on to its essential worth, Schumpeter is closer to Ricardo than to Marx.[11] She says

> although the terminology and background are entirely different, and explicit doctrines play the same part as Ricardo's hints and loose ends, the similarity is unmistakable. Ricardo holds, like Schumpeter that any economic system works on the law of the static state, i.e. that incomes, prices and real costs determine each other; instead of taking the Marxian line of establishing the complete validity of the real costs or labour theory of value by making it more and more abstract, he allows it to exist in the real world 'considerably modified'.
>
> (Warriner, 1931: 47)

Some commentators (for example, Hodgson, 1993) have questioned whether Schumpeter ever managed to integrate successfully the two seemingly incompatible strands of his economic theory – statics and equilibrium on the one hand and dynamics and disequilibrium on the other. They point to the fact that Chapters 1 and 2 of his *Theory of*

Economic Development (1934) are juxtaposed, but not integrated. Hodgson (1993: 150) says that Schumpeter's 'own conception of evolution forms an adjunct of Walrasian equilibrium, and represents an ostensible but ultimately unsatisfactory attempt to reconcile general equilibrium theory with notions of variety and change' (quoted in Maneschi, 2000: 5). This dualism of theory can be seen to influence Schumpeter's conception and discussion of leadership, when he makes a distinction between businessmen of average abilities who carry out routine economic activities of the circular flow, and entrepreneurs who develop new combinations (resultant from, and necessary to manage, disequilibrium). Schumpeter's conception of leadership, and indeed his whole economic analysis, is underpinned by his unique vision of economic progress.

Schumpeter's vision

The term vision is so closely associated with Schumpeter that comparisons between his vision and the vision of other economists are inevitably prone to specific ontological bias, so that we tend to view other visions in a way that filters our understanding according to Schumpeterian analysis (Maneschi, 2000). Schumpeter himself took the view that the importance of vision depended on the nature of the problem being addressed and that in some cases, such as when we are concerned with how economic quantities hang together (as in Ricardian economics), the role of vision is a modest one (Prendergast, 2006: 253).

Schumpeter defined vision as 'a pre-analytic cognitive act' necessary 'to visualise a distinct set of coherent phenomena' (which in this case was a history of economic analysis) (Schumpeter and Schumpeter, 1954: 41). He referred to vision as 'this way of our mind' and explicitly equated vision with ideology when he said, 'now it should be perfectly clear that there is a wide gate for ideology to enter into this process. In fact, it enters on the very ground floor, into the pre-analytical act of which we are speaking. Analytical work begins with material provided by our vision of things, and this vision is ideological almost by definition' (1954: 42).

But what was Schumpeter's vision? Prendergast (2006: 253) says that its essence might be summed up as 'the idea ... that reality, as we know it from experience, may be in itself an evolutionary process, evolving from inherent necessity, instead of being a set of phenomena that seek a definite state or level, so that an extraneous factor ... is necessary in order to move them to another state or level' (Schumpeter and Schumpeter, 1954: 437). This vision of the process of economic development should be distinguished from Schumpeter's vision of the outcome of that process – the implosion of capitalism and its replacement by socialism – with which he is also associated (see, for example, Heertje, 1981). Whereas Schumpeter's vision of the outcomes of economic development is most relevant to sociologists, his vision of the process of economic development is most relevant to economists.

Schumpeter was concerned to construct 'a theoretical model of the process of economic change in time … to answer the question how the economic system generates the force which incessantly transforms it' (Clemence, 1951: 158–159, quoted in Prendergast, 2006: 254). He admired Walras's account of an economic system of equilibrium which, while not entirely stationary, did not change 'of itself' but merely adapted itself to natural and social influences acting on it. Schumpeter felt that this was an inadequate explanation of the reality of economic development. Rather, he defined development as 'such changes in economic life as are not forced upon it from without but arise by its own initiative from within' (1934: 65). This involved spontaneous and discontinuous change and disturbance of the equilibrium. This change invariably came from producers rather than consumers of final products.[12] It involved the introduction of new goods or methods of production, the opening of new markets, new sources of supply or the fundamental reorganisation of a particular industry.

Such endogenous change was the work of entrepreneurs, who carried out many 'new combinations' of enterprise. Entrepreneurs alone could exploit all the new possibilities that discontinuous change presented. Whereas individuals (managers) could act promptly and rationally under the system of equilibrium, because tasks were routine and well understood, when discontinuous change occurred they were uncertain how to proceed. Past experience, custom and practice were actually a hindrance to progress. A great effort was required to break out of this way of thinking, in order to be able to create the new combinations which the new economic reality demanded. Few individuals were capable of this effort of will in addition to their normal tasks (Prendergast, 2006).

It was entrepreneurs who were able to create these new combinations and to put them into action. Schumpeter's entrepreneur was motivated by 'the will to found a private kingdom, usually, though not necessarily, also a dynasty … the will to conquer, the impulse to fight, to prove oneself superior to others, to succeed for the sake, not for the fruits of success itself … the joy of creating, of getting things done, or simply of exercising one's energy and ingenuity' (Schumpeter, 1934: 93). Yet, it was the implementation that was key 'it is this "doing the thing", without which possibilities are dead, of which the leader's function consists ... leadership ... does not consist of finding or creating the new thing but in so impressing the social group with it as to draw it on its wake. It is therefore, more by will than by intellect that leaders fulfil their function' (ibid.: 88).

Leadership and entrepreneurship

Schumpeter described entrepreneurship as 'a special case of the social phenomenon of leadership' (Schumpeter, 1928) and the two terms cannot be separated for any practicable purposes in his writings. However, 'the relation between entrepreneurship and general leadership is a very complex one and lends itself to a number of misunderstandings' (Schumpeter, 1951: 254; Prendergast, 2006: 259). Schumpeter acknowledged that misunderstandings of his earlier works made necessary revisions to his theory. As Prendergast has pointed out,

> leadership was a core concept in all of Schumpeter's writings on development but the content of the concept underwent considerable change over time. These changes were in part a response to the changing nature of the capitalist enterprise and the wider capitalist system. They also reflected development in Schumpeter's own thought and his responses to the work by Usher and other economic historians on the history of innovation.
>
> (Prendergast, 2006: 266)

Schumpeter has been criticised for being elitist, particularly in his earlier works. Santarelli and Pesciarelli (1990: 689) contend that, 'it is possible to argue that the overall vision of Schumpeter's two early works has elements in common with the philosophy of Friedrich Nietzsche'. That is, Schumpeter's sub-division of individuals into an elite he named entrepreneurs able to develop new combinations of the means of production, and businessmen of average abilities who carry out routine economic activities of the circular flow, can be compared with Nietzsche's division of humans into 'overmen' and the 'mass' or 'herd'. Santarelli and Pesciarelli conclude that this underpins Schumpeter's entire vision of development and that 'the separateness of the static and dynamic worlds on which Schumpeter dwells at such length springs from the separateness of the two types of human being that the two worlds underlie' (ibid.: 691).[13] Elsewhere, Maerz (1991) has compared Schumpeter's analysis with the elitist theories of Tarde, Dilthey and Pareto.

However, Prendergast (2006) has shown, in a carefully considered analysis of Schumpeter's writings on leadership, and citing the interpretations of De Vecchi (1995), Shionoya (1996) and Swedberg (1991) that, although accusations of elitism may be justified by Schumpeter's earlier writings, such accusations cannot be sustained in light of the development and moderation of his views on leadership in subsequent years. She concludes, 'Schumpeter's concept of leadership was never entirely heroic or devoid of sociological content, but over time, greater emphasis came to be placed on the interaction between the leader and the socio-economic circumstances of which the leader himself was the product' (2006: 266).

Indeed, we can identify in Prendergast's analysis a number of positions that Schumpeter took which, taken together, suggest a more recognisably modern theory of leadership.

- By the 1934 English translation of his *Theory of Economic Development*, and in contrast to the first edition of 1911, the sharp division of men into static and dynamic types was abandoned. Instead Schumpeter suggested that entrepreneurial capacity would be normally distributed in an ethnically homogeneous group. Some would be good, some would be bad and some indifferent. Schumpeter recognised that the entrepreneurial function need not be embodied in a physical person and in particular in a single physical person (Schumpeter, 1951). He noted that the Department of Agriculture had revolutionised the practice of farmers in the United States and, with the development of large-scale corporations, the entrepreneurial function was filled cooperatively to a greater and greater extent (Swedberg, 1991: 172–173; Prendergast, 2006: 261).
- Schumpeter compared the role and attributes of the family entrepreneur with those of the manager or official in corporate industry. The family entrepreneur had to have energy and focus but the corporate entrepreneur also needed consummate skill to be able to win support and to negotiate. Here political connections and articulateness were vital assets (Schumpeter, 1951: 161–162).
- Schumpeter said that it was easy to overestimate the autonomy and importance of the individual, and in later writings he appears to become increasingly sensitive to the limits imposed on the leader's sphere of activity. He wrote, 'mankind is not free to choose … things economic and social move by their own momentum and the ensuing situations compel individuals and groups to behave in certain ways whatever they may wish to do, not indeed by

destroying their freedom of choice but by shaping the choosing mentalities and by narrowing the list of possibilities from which to choose' (Schumpeter, 1947: 129–130).

• In contrast to the idea of the great man (often characterised in military or political leadership), Schumpeter's leader did not stand outside or above his sphere of activity. The entrepreneur achieved control over production, not by virtue of personal charisma or of being selected (by the masses) to fulfil this role, but through normal productive activity.

• Finally, although the leader should have vision, 'the capacity of seeing things in a way which afterwards proves to be true, even though it cannot be established in a moment, and of grasping the essential fact, discarding the unessential, even though one can give no account of the principles by which this is done' (Schumpeter, 1934: 265–285) it is also clear that the effectiveness of Schumpeter's entrepreneur can only be judged *post factum*. Leaders will be judged by their results.

These refinements to his thinking, although significant, do not detract from Schumpeter's fundamental distinction between 'mere managers' and 'entrepreneurs'. Schumpeter did not have much interest in the former, or at least he had no more regard for such managers than for ordinary workers because 'the function of superintendence in itself, constitutes no essential economic distinction' and 'the mere circumstance that ranks one worker above another worker in the industrial organisation, in a directing and superintending position, does not make his labour into something distinct' (Schumpeter, 1955: 20). He continues, 'insofar as individuals in their economic conduct simply draw conclusions from known circumstances – and that indeed is what we are here dealing with and what economics has always dealt with – it is no significance whether they are directing or directed' (ibid.: 21).

Winter (2006: 136) summarises Schumpeter's view of mere management as 'in short, the manager of a firm, when the economic system is in an equilibrium circular flow, is just another guy who knows his job in a firm full of people who know their jobs', and Schumpeter himself draws a sharp distinction between mere management and entrepreneurship when he writes, 'carrying out a new plan and acting according to a customary one are things as different as making a road and walking along it' (Schumpeter, 1955: 85).

Although Schumpeter's vision was predicated on leadership, and he wrote directly about different aspects of leadership and entrepreneurship, including, latterly, the role of leadership in large firms, he did not fully develop his theories in a specific organisational context. This was left to Penrose (1959) whose important contribution we shall discuss shortly.

Innovation and technology

Schumpeter recognised that 'short wave' innovation created during equilibrium was capable of producing economic rents either through resource differentials or through imperfections in the market. He acknowledged that monopolistic positions are often positive for economic development because they create the environment through which big firms take risks and innovate. This acknowledgement is often taken to mean that Schumpeter was concerned with innovation within equilibrium – or, more precisely, during temporary disruptions to equilibrium when monopolistic positions are created – rather than with innovation at disequilibrium.

Rosenberg (2000: 6) is unequivocal in his rejection of such an interpretation when he says that 'Schumpeter's analysis of innovation is fundamentally a disequilibrium analysis, which continually (or, more precisely intermittently) burst out of the confines of static equilibrium analysis'. Further, the literature on the 'Schumpeterian hypothesis' involves a misreading of Part II of *Capitalism, Socialism and Democracy* because 'Schumpeter was not arguing that monopoly is the most congenial market environment for innovation. His argument, rather, was that innovation commonly creates monopoly, but these monopolies are only temporary – mere epiphenomena thrown up by the inherent technological dynamism of advanced capitalist economies. Schumpeter's deeper point, so brilliantly sketched out in Chapter 7 (The Process of Creative Destruction) is that the inability of static equilibrium analysis to capture the essential long-term features of capitalist reality' (2000: 7). As we shall see in the next chapter, such misinterpretation of Schumpeter in the 'Schumpeterian hypothesis' underpins much strategic management thinking.

Schumpeter was concerned with 'long wave' innovation where innovation was the engine of economic development and wealth creation. Capitalism is an evolutionary system based upon the essential forces of pursuit of profits, incentive structure and nature of competition. This is not mere price competition, but competition from the 'new commodity, the new technology, the new source of supply, the new type of organisation' (Schumpeter, 1942: 84–85). Economic change is the very essence of capitalism. Capitalism is not, and never can be, stationary. Indeed, 'stationary capitalism is a contradiction in terms'

(Rosenberg, 2000: 15). The main agency for change in capitalism is innovation. Innovation is more than technological innovation, but technological innovation is vital to long-term economic growth.

Schumpeter (like Marx, but in contrast to most economists of his time) regarded innovation – and science and technology – as endogenous. That is, innovation, science and technology are the products of the incentive mechanism of capitalism and associated bourgeois culture. They are subject to the economic forces and 'habits of mind' which these involve. Therefore innovation, and science and technology are not exogenous factors, and they are not independent factors, since they 'were just as much the product of the bourgeois class culture – hence, ultimately, of the business class – as was the business performance itself' (quoted in Rosenberg, 2000: 11).[14]

Rosenberg makes the important point that innovation (and science and technology) does not result only from present-day culture and intellect but also is a product of history, as each generation is shaped by, and builds upon, cultural and intellectual inheritance derived from previous generations. So innovation (and science and technology) is endogenous also in a historical context to the extent that what was valued in the past is valued in the present. A practical manifestation of such historical endogeneity can be found in the tendency of firms to invest in proven technologies, and to emphasise development over research, imitation over innovation.

Rosenberg (2000) draws a clear line between the work of Schumpeter (and Marx) and New Growth Theory (e.g. Romer, 1990) by interpreting endogenous change in its broadest sense 'In the context of economic discussions, I mean by "endogenous" that certain outcomes (e.g., the availability of new technologies) need to be understood as the result of purposive actions undertaken by decision makers who are responding to market forces in the pursuit of profit maximisation' (Rosenberg, 2000: 107). Following this broader interpretation, we argue that the adoption and implementation of information technology is also endogenous because these actions are also the result of decision makers responding to prevailing economic conditions.

As Cantwell (2000: 11) points out, a problem with the original formulation of Schumpeter's theory of innovation is that it is predicated on the separation of innovation and imitation and on the ability to identify the original source of innovation. In fact, because of greater technological complexity within and between firms, it has become increasingly difficult to distinguish between innovation and imitation, as innovation invariably incorporates some elements of imitation, and imitation requires absorptive capacity that comes from innovation. This makes separating innovators from imitators very difficult. Schumpeter believed that innovation profits should go to the innovators but in practice it is far from clear how innovation profits should be distributed.

It is becoming increasingly clear that the first mover in a successful innovation does not always perform best. Although among large firms technological leaders tend to retain leadership positions from one phase of development to the next, at the level of the industry, the level of innovative profits and technology-based growth is determined by the speed at which other firms catch up (Cantwell and Andersen, 1996). This suggests that innovative profits are created by followers and not just by leaders. In addition, technological leaders are not in general the firms that earn the highest profits within the industry or experience the most rapid growth (Teece, 1992; Andersen and Cantwell, 1999).

In the evolutionary theory of technological change (Nelson and Winter, 1982; Rosenberg, 1982), innovation success is determined in large part by the ability to transfer innovation from one context to another. This, in turn, is determined by the degree of technological readiness or complementarity between activities (Cantwell and Barrera, 1998) and the degree of absorptive capacity in the recipient or imitating firm (Cohen and Levinthal, 1989). This is not necessarily or even usually the case with the first mover. Often it is follower firms who have the best fit between an innovation and existing capabilities. As we shall see in the next chapter, this important observation informed the development of the Resource Based Theory (Penrose, 1959; Barney, 1991).

Rosenberg (2000) argues that Schumpeter appears to have had little interest in the post-innovation improvement process (though he would not have denied its economic importance). Rather, 'his vision and his sociology led him to insist upon the sharp distinction between invention and innovation, on the one hand, and between innovation and imitation on the other' (2000: 63). He attached too much importance to the first introduction of innovation into the marketplace, and not enough importance to how that innovation was subsequently imitated. This was over-simplistic and created an expectation about the productive impact of innovations that was unrealistic. This, at least in part, explains the IT productivity paradox: we expect too much of technology, too soon and too often.

According to Rosenberg there are a number of reasons why technological change and innovation do not (apparently) produce concomitant productivity growth. It takes time – a lot longer than we generally are prepared to allow for – maybe the entire lifespan of the technology. A new technology takes time to get right (it was 30 years from the first flight by the Wright brothers until the commercialisation of flight with the advent of the DC10). It takes society time to adopt and adapt the new technology (e.g. 3G messaging). It can be very difficult to measure some productivity benefits, particularly those in the service sector. For example, it is relatively easy to measure cost reductions or output additions in a manufacturing environment but much more difficult to measure and account for the impact of the greater availability and quality of services. So when we observe the productivity paradox, particularly as it relates to IT ('we see the computer everywhere except in the productivity statistics': Robert Solow, quoted by Rosenberg, 2000: 59), we may simply be observing a delay and difficulty in accounting for technological change.

A related problem is measuring the wrong thing – measuring what we can (or what is easy to) measure rather than what should be measured, and important improvements can be missed. For example, productivity improvements are more difficult to measure in the service industry, which is the fastest growing sector of the economy and a sector of significant technological investment, yet much of the consumer surplus is unaccounted for and there is not even a clear definition of what constitutes output (Rosenberg, 2000: 74). Adding to the difficulty is the fact that productivity improvements may extend beyond the original technology itself, beyond the hardware or software, to include non-technology factors such as customer service, employee morale and stakeholder satisfaction. Technology may play a part in such improvements within a resource bundle of strategic assets. Therefore we need to look beyond Schumpeter (but still with a Schumpeterian perspective), and beyond the productivity impact of innovations, to the productivity impact of imitations.

To the extent that technologies develop into general-purpose technologies, they rely on complementarity and imitation. Complementarity occurs when two technologies combined produce greater benefit than either does alone.[15] The synergy between the electronic digital computer and the integrated circuit is one good example of such complementarity, since this paved the way (by replacing the old vacuum tube) for the development of the modern computer industry. Another example is the use of fibre optics and the laser which has led to vast improvement in the speed and quality of communications. These are specific examples from a general canon that includes the steam engine, machine tools, and electricity. Each technology has created complementarities with other technologies and has been exploited beyond the initial introduction of the innovation through successive imitations. However, benefits beyond the introduction of the base technology have taken time to realise.

The direct benefits arising from the introduction of electricity were realised in a relatively short period of time (about 40 years), but the indirect benefits accruing through the complementarity of electricity with other technologies, and involving many successive innovations and imitations (for example in steel, metallurgy and aluminium), took much longer. These developments, and others, relied on the development of the electricity infrastructure which secured and regulated electricity supply, and which itself was the result of successive innovations and imitations. Similarly, the computer has undergone significant modifications and improvements since it was first introduced in recognisably modern form in 1945, and continues to do so. In fact, the internet may be seen as merely one in a long line of developments that have leveraged the power of the base general purpose technology. In this sense, we should not be too impatient to measure the benefits of IT. Many benefits accruing from the application of electricity to iron, steel and aluminium production were not measurable until long after the base technology had been introduced. There is no reason to believe that IT will be any different. Indeed, the greater complexity of IT suggests that this will take much longer.

Technology (along with science and innovation) is an endogenous factor of production. Rosenberg (2000: 4) points to two propositions which Schumpeter (1942) called 'invaluable working hypotheses' to substantiate this view. The first is that 'forms of production are the fundamental determinant of social structures which in turn breed attitudes, action and civilisation'. The second is that 'the forms of production themselves have a logic of their own; that is to say, they change according to necessities inherent in them so as to produce their successors merely by their own working' (ibid.: 4).

Rosenberg (2000: 25) later cites a number of examples of technological endogeneity. These include the rise of industrial research labs, the public funding of science and technology through specific research institutes, and the myriad professional and business associations, with their journals, conferences, annual meetings and standing committees. He observes that most research and development spending goes to improve existing technologies, in a rough proportion of one-third research to two-thirds development. This is endogeneity in resource allocation. Resource allocation today is determined by previous resource allocation and successes. Examples include the transistor radio, automobile, aircraft, camera, electricity and telephone: 'that is to say, what we are observing is a process in which successful earlier investments in inventive activities have created economic incentives that have generated many years of further investment in product improvement. These later investments which now appear to dominate the R&D budget of advanced capitalist economies, are thus clearly endogenous in their nature' (2000: 28).

Of particular importance has been the role of engineering disciplines in applying and commercialising science and technology and linking science and technology research directly to economic incentives. Engineering disciplines illustrate how downstream applications of science and technology can lead to further investment in upstream scientific research, as the benefits of the application and commercialisation of initial research activities become apparent. Examples here include iron and steel smelting, paper making and instrumentation.

Penrose (1959) was the first to develop the implications of Schumpeter's thoughts on technology for the firm. Technology enables firms to leverage their resources and capabilities to develop long-term sustainable profits through innovation. Technology facilitates the collaborative knowledge flows and learning which make this possible. Schumpeter (and Penrose) saw technology as locally embedded and in this he (and she) appears not to have predicted the internet (which is global and ubiquitous). However, Schumpeter and Penrose were not referring to the base technology, but to that bundle of resources which the technology made possible. It was this resource bundle which included technology and other capabilities and competencies that was local and embedded because it was based on specialisation, learning and historic path dependency. Such differentiated and heterogeneous resource bundles can be difficult, if not impossible, to replicate elsewhere.

Winter (2006) reflects the extent of this difficulty (and the approach to its solution in management theories of core competencies, complementarities and absorptive capacities) when he writes:

> as Schumpeter's statement on the introduction of new methods of production suggests, the difficulties standing in the way of adaptive or innovative change have little to do with the newness of the technique in a scientific sense, or indeed in any sense that abstracts from the details of the situation in which change occurs. They have to do with the fragmentation of relevant knowledge, both of operations and concepts, and with the degree to which some existing, functioning organisation provides a solution to the problem of fitting the fragments together.
>
> (2006: 138)

Technology in general and IT in particular make possible new combinations, for example international collaborations, and IT enables firms to extend their technological diversification. IT has been described as a 'carrier branch' or 'transmission belt' for the transfer of innovation across sectors (Rosenberg, 1976; Freeman and Perez, 1988). IT is a 'core connector' of technological development, not only passing information and knowledge between disparate fields but actually combining these fields. So pervasive has IT become that 'it is not leadership in IT as such that is likely to count for most, but rather the capacity to blend IT with other technologies as a means of fusing them together and creating new combinations' (Cantwell, 2000: 21). The implications of this conclusion, and its antecedent economic assumptions, are now discussed.

Conclusion

Cantwell (2000) makes the important point that Schumpeter's theory of profit and growth through innovation has itself been appropriated by 'the standard interpretation' found in the literature which casts Schumpeter's theory inside conventional market-based analysis. Here innovation is a means to achieve quasi-monopoly position and super-profits through first-mover advantages. Cantwell concludes:

> in other words the standard treatment reduces the means through which profits can be earned through innovation to a matter of the capacity for static appropriability through the exercise of market power, and hence analytically no different to any other kind of 'normal' profits. The relevant markets may be new, but their newness is significant only for its relationship to the scope of temporary monopolies. The distinctiveness of Schumpeter's notion of adding to the existing circular flow is lost.
>
> (2000: 3)

Thus the standard interpretation, which became known as the 'Schumpeterian hypothesis' is quite different from Schumpeter's original theory which emphasised the role of entrepreneurship and the seeking out of opportunities for new-value generating activities that would expand and transform the circular flow of income. Cantwell argues (2000: 7) that this misinterpretation is understandable because those making it did so from the limitations of the conventional (or Ricardian) theory of competition.

In fact Schumpeter made a distinction between two realms of economic analysis, and two different means for creating profits. The first realm was traditional economic theory based upon the circular flow of income, where profits are derived from market power (or market imperfections) which distort the circular flow of income, acting upon prices and quantities in the market, to the advantage of one or a few firms. The second realm is one which augments the circular flow of income through innovation, creativity and change. Market power still exists but only as a coincidental by-product of the unevenness of the creative process. The real source of profits is the creative process that adds new wealth to the income stream.

It was left to Penrose (1959) to apply these two different streams of economic analysis to the firm. The firm is a price and output decision-taker which can earn higher profits through increasing its market power. But the firm is also a device for innovation, problem solving and learning. Penrose suggested that the first realm could be left to the conventional theory of the firm, but the second realm required a separate theory of the growth of the firm, 'so long as it cultivates its own garden, we cultivate ours' (Penrose, 1959: 10). In this she reflects Schumpeter. Profit maximisation through market-based allocation and co-ordination of resources could be explained within Walrasian equilibrium, but profit seeking through innovation could not.

The appropriation and misinterpretation of Schumpeter's theory by traditional market-based analysis may have been encouraged by Schumpeter's change of position on the role of innovation as a result of the growth of R and D in large firms. In his original theory (1911 and 1934) Schumpeter emphasised the role of entrepreneurship in value-generating activities which would expand the circular flow of income. He made a distinction between invention or discovery on the one hand and innovation, commercialisation and entrepreneurship on the other (effectively reflecting the nineteenth-century institutional model of innovation, wherein independent inventors offered their inventions to entrepreneurs for commercialisation).

However, by 1954 Schumpeter had changed his emphasis to large oligolistic firms in which invention and innovation, discovery and commercialisation, research and development, took place hand in hand. Because these big firms exercised excessive market power, the connection was made between innovation and market power in what became known as the 'Schumpeterian hypothesis'. As Cantwell (2002) makes clear, this connection and hypothesis formed no part of Schumpeter's original theory.[16] So while Schumpeter reflected the rise of in-house research and development that accompanied the publication of *History of Economic Analysis* in 1954, he did not change his original theory to make a connection between innovation and monopoly rents. Moreover, as Cantrell points out, Schumpeter did not fully develop the implications of his theory of innovation for large firms (this was left to Penrose, 1959).

In addition to developing the implication of Schumpeter's theory for the firm, Penrose (1959) is credited with providing the foundations for what became known as the resource-based view (RBV) of the firm. A full discussion of RBV will appear in the next chapter. At this juncture, it is sufficient to note that Penrose's work has also been misunderstood, misinterpreted and misappropriated. It is true that in her discussion of resource-based heterogeneity among firms Penrose laid the foundations for the RBV, but she also sought to emphasise the radical implications of Schumpeter's original theory on innovation. So whereas Penrose is often cited in support of the RBV, the RBV itself is often discussed in support of the Schumpeterian hypothesis and market-based analysis. As we shall argue in the next chapter, it is left for the development of the concept of dynamic capabilities (Teece *et al.*, 1997; Eisenhardt and Martin, 2000) to fully realise the implications of Penrose's analysis of Schumpeter's theory.

Although Cantwell (2000, 2002) makes a strong case for the re-casting of Schumpeter's legacy according to the power of his original theory, he acknowledges that Schumpeter's theory requires to be updated to fit the modern context. Again Penrose provides an excellent foundation by 'explicitly incorporating the role of in-house R&D and endogenous innovation in large firms and by anticipating the recent approach to technological change and the firm with her resource based perspective on corporate growth' (Cantwell, 2000: 4). He argues that recent developments have increased the value of Schumpeter's original theory. These include the growing importance of innovation profits relative to traditional profits derived from market power, the increasing importance of organisational learning, flexibility, technological change and diversification, collaboration, networks, shared capabilities, and internationalisation. These reflect a shift away from obtaining profits through exploitation of market power towards the creation of innovative profits through new capabilities.

Like Schumpeter, Penrose acknowledged that firms could innovate to maximise profits and to exploit market power to achieve monopoly rents. But this was quite different from innovating by using resources and capabilities to achieve long-term growth. 'Examples of growth over long periods which can be attributed exclusively to such protection [market power] are rare, although elements of such protection are to be found in the position of nearly every large firm' (Penrose, 1959: 113, quoted in Cantwell, 2000: 14).

In any case, the use of innovation within existing market structures – for example developing technological expertise or the use of marketing and advertising to create new opportunities – would be limited by the market itself, and would not necessarily be transferable to other markets. Much better for the firm to concentrate on building technological competence because 'in the long run the profitability, survival and growth of the firm does not depend so much on the efficiency with which it is able to organise the production of even a widely diversified range of products as it does on the ability of the firm to establish one or more wide and relatively impregnable bases from which it can adapt and extend its operations in an uncertain, changing and competitive world' (Penrose, 1959: 137).[17]

So a firm needed to develop resources and capabilities that allowed it to diversify beyond its current markets and operations. Developing such a capability created a virtuous circle for the firm, as it was able not only to exploit existing opportunities, but to 'see' or anticipate new ones. In this Penrose anticipated the development of the concept of absorptive capacity (Cohen and Levinthal, 1989). Although not explicitly addressed by Penrose, it should be clear also that the reverse situation is true. A firm that does not develop such a capability will fail not only to exploit existing market opportunities but also to identify new ones. This then becomes a vicious circle as such a firm, without taking corrective action, becomes increasing uncompetitive. A key factor here is the firm's willingness and ability to learn. As we shall demonstrate later in this book (Chapter 5), in small firms, where the role of the owner-manager is key, virtuous and vicious cycles can be explained by the theory of enactment.

Echoing Schumpeter, Penrose observes that although the application of particular capabilities may be quick and conclusive, the development of these capabilities in the actual creative process is slow. Such competences evolve gradually and change slowly and much less dramatically because their development involves learning. Therein lies the key to the survival of large firms. 'The Schumpeterian process of creative destruction has not destroyed the large firm, on the contrary, it has forced it to become more and more creative. When it (the firm) develops a specialised knowledge of a technology which is not itself very specific to any kind of product it enables at least the large firm to turn aside the process of creative destruction and to thrive on the novelty which might otherwise have destroyed it' (Penrose, 1959: 22–23).

Penrose's contribution is summed up by Cantwell (2000): 'what is interesting [here] is not just her linking of Schumpeter's [second realm] of innovative profits to the resource-based theory of growth of the firm, but also the way in which, as a result, she depicted the direction of corporate learning and growth as a path dependent resource-constrained process' and in this respect she 'anticipated current ideas on the evolutionary approach to technological change, and in particular the notions of corporate technological trajectories (Dosi, 1982), corporate technological diversification (Pavitt, Robson and Townsend, 1989; Granstrand and Sjolander, 1990, Granstrand, Patel and Pavitt, 1997) and corporate coherence in diversification (Teece, Dosi, Rumelt and Winter, 1994)' (2000: 16).

As Cantwell concludes, Penrose gave practical application to the ideas of Schumpeter. The importance of innovation to long-term profits and growth of the firm is notable (as opposed to profits from market power); technological competition becomes more intense, firms are forced to specialise (due to practical resource constraints) and focus on clusters of related capabilities within (and between) firms. In doing so, she anticipated the increasing relevance of Schumpeter's ideas, and her own application of them, in today's business context, where it is much more difficult to establish and sustain positions of market power, given intense international competition and technological complexity and where economies of scale and scope are reduced because of increasing market sophistication and diversification, forcing firms to specialise in increasingly more narrowly defined product markets, which require significant investment, and therefore firms cannot as easily compete across a portfolio of products and markets.

In the final analysis, although Penrose performed an invaluable service in translating Schumpeter's economic theory to the level of the firm, her work has not had the impact it might (or indeed should) have had. This is due largely to the aforementioned misunderstanding, misinterpretation and misappropriation of her (and Schumpeter's) economic analysis in the form of the 'Schumpeterian hypothesis'. This, and its consequences, provides a subtext for our next chapter.

3   IT and management theory

Introduction

In the previous chapter, a duality of Schumpeter's theory was identified. This duality is evident in Schumpeter's division of the economic world into equilibrium and disequilibrium and in his distinction between management and entrepreneurship. Schumpeter's theory is grounded in a duality of equilibrium and disequilibrium, not in their dichotomy. He did not reject equilibrium, nor did he deny the important role played by managers within it. Rather, he was concerned with its limitation and sought to explore what happened when equilibrium broke down. At such times 'mere' management must give way to entrepreneurship, leadership and innovation. This was when and where Schumpeterian rents were created. In this chapter, the duality in Schumpeter's theory is discussed in the context of the strategic management literature. Schumpeter's duality has been ignored by many management thinkers. In particular the origins and impact of the 'Schumpeterian hypothesis' – that innovation is essentially a function of imperfection in market structure and therefore a feature of equilibrium rather than of disequilibrium – is discussed.

Resource-based theory (more commonly known as the resource-based view or RBV) is introduced. The application of this theory, which is the pre-eminent theory of competition in the strategic management literature, reflects the underlying confusion of the Schumpeterian hypothesis. Because of Penrose's emphasis on resources and capabilities, and her close association with Schumpeterian theory, RBV has appropriated Schumpeter's theory. In RBV, innovation is often confined to conditions of static equilibrium and market power. We argue that RBV is essentially a Ricardian theory best suited to conditions of static or relatively static equilibrium and therefore not applicable to the kind of volatile situations Schumpeter suggested at disequilibrium. The true inheritor of Schumpeterian theory is dynamic capabilities. Dynamic capabilities share many features of RBV,[1] but the terms are not synonymous. Dynamic capabilities are most useful to managers operating in turbulent environments.

The implications of this conclusion for IT and competitive advantage are explored. From economic theory we conclude that IT is a resource and a capability operating in static and dynamic environments, a direct and indirect influence on firm performance. IT is the subject of 'mere' management and of leadership, of innovation and entrepreneurship. We look for evidence of these conclusions in the strategic management literature. We examine empirical studies of the direct and indirect impact of IT as a strategic asset (comprising resources and capabilities) on firm performance. We introduce the concept of complementarity and discuss the role of IT as an enabler of other strategic assets. First, however, we provide some background context by briefly examining the relationship between economic theory and strategic management research.

Economic theory and strategic management research

Lockett and Thompson (2001), although concerned with the impact of RBV on economics (and not with the impact of economics on the RBV), acknowledge the strong links between economics and strategy in general. They say

> not merely does strategy share with two of the principal fields in economics, industrial organisation (IO) and financial economics, a central concern with the processes determining firm performance, but it draws heavily upon economic models of firm behaviour. This is most obviously seen in the influence of the Structure–Conduct–Performance (SCP) paradigm, rooted in the work of Bain (1968) and most clearly articulated in the strategy context by Michael Porter (1980, 1985). Furthermore, the RBV itself is rooted in insights from economics, such as those of Penrose (1959), Richardson (1972) and Teece (1980), and has been developed by individual scholars, many of whom have made significant contributions in the economics literature and in some cases continue to do so. Moreover, much of the empirical research using firm level data, published in economics and strategy journals, exhibits a considerable overlap in methodology and research questions, not surprisingly since many researchers publish in both areas.
>
> (Lockett and Thompson, 2001: 724–725)

Surprisingly, neither Ricardo nor Schumpeter, nor indeed any economist, are mentioned, although those who have developed economic theories at firm level, and are here regarded as economists, including Penrose, Teece and Williamson, are acknowledged.[2]

Mathews (2006) is unequivocal on the relationship between economic theory and management strategy. He draws upon the work of Frank Knight (1942) to identify three ways in which firms can potentially earn profits. In perfectly competitive markets, profits and rents are zero, and all strategising behaviour has ceased. He notes that, 'while this position in economic space is of overwhelming significance for microeconomics, it is of zero significance for strategizing'; that 'constructions such as the neoclassical theory of the firm that are built on such foundations have little to teach business scholars' and that this is 'no place for strategizing behaviour as understood by business schools'. The second position is one of imperfectly competitive equilibrium where profits (and Ricardian rents) may be earned due to restrictions on competition (as in the Industrial Organisation tradition) or due to restricted mobility of resources (as in mainstream RBV): 'in such a perspective, rents arise from frictions or imperfections in the economy, and strategizing is reduced to the search for such imperfections'. Finally there is disequilibrium. Here 'Knightian profits can be earned through firms taking entrepreneurial initiatives, such as capturing increasing returns from reorganizing their activities (as in outsourcing) or from the capture of resource complementarities, or from learning effects'. This is 'the most general position' that 'most firms find themselves in, for most of the time' (Mathews, 2006: 103–104).

Mathews (2006) credits Knight with two pieces of 'intellectual deck cleaning' which paved the way for 'a powerful theory that lies behind all serious discussion of profits in economic textbooks [that] has never been surpassed'. First, he introduced a fundamental distinction between risk, which can be estimated according to a known probability distribution, and can be observed and, at least in principle, insured against, and uncertainty. He then linked these distinctions to a notion of profit which he defined as pure residual income, that is, income after all contractual payments for factors utilised have been made. This 'cleared up the endless debates of the nineteenth century over whether profit should include interest, or wages of management, or a return to the fourth factor of production' (ibid.: 102).

Knight then identified residual earnings with the irreducible uncertainty that attaches to every business enterprise. This in turn cleared away previous confusion over whether profits arose only as a result of dynamics or innovation (the Schumpeterian position), or could result from disturbances of the price system (the Ricardian, classical and neo classical position). According to Knight, in so far as risks can be insured against, they cannot share in the residual, and therefore profit (as a residual) accrues to the bearer of uncertainty, which is the entrepreneur (considered either as an individual or as a firm). Contractual incomes can mitigate the effects of risk, but not of uncertainty. 'Thus Knight reconciled his vision with neowalrasian orthodoxy, which holds that at equilibrium, all excess earnings, i.e. non contractual earnings, are reduced to zero' (Mathews, 2006: 102).[3]

Mathews claims that Knight's theory that profits constitute a residual category of income corresponding to the irreducible uncertainty associated with a business enterprise 'is an unshakeable feature of modern economic reasoning', that it 'saves entrepreneurship from its extinction at the hands of general equilibrium theory', and that it reveals that 'true uncertainty about the future might allow entrepreneurial firms to earn positive profits despite perfect competition and long-run equilibrium'. He concludes: 'thus the implications of Knight's theory of profits are profound, and not apparently widely understood in the economics community nor within the strategic management community, where arguably it has most relevance' (ibid.: 102).

Mathews places RBV and industrial organisation (IO) theories together under imperfectly competitive equilibrium, and does not regard RBV operating in conditions of disequilibrium, and therefore a logical extension of Schumpeterian economics (and of Penrose's theory of the firm). Thereby he firmly rejects the Schumpeterian hypothesis which (as we have already argued) 'reduces the means through which profits can be earned through innovation to a matter of capacity for static appropriability through the exercise of markets power, and hence analytically no different to any other kind of normal profits' (Cantwell, 2000: 3).[4]

The significance of this interpretation of Schumpeter's economic theory for management is important not only because it identifies where strategy may be most effective but also because it emphasises those aspects of management that most contribute to that strategy – leadership, innovation and entrepreneurship.

The resource-based view

The resource-based view (RBV) has its origin in Penrose's (1959) conception of the firm as a bundle of resources that grows through the exploitation of these resources. Her ideas were developed by Rubin (1973), Wernerfelt (1984), Barney (1986a; 1986b) and Prahalad and

Hamel (1990). It is Barney (1991) who is credited with 'the first formulation of the then fragmented resource based literature into a comprehensive (and thus empirically feasible) theoretical framework' (Newbert, 2007: 123). Levitas and Ndofor (2006) consider RBV to be the dominant or guiding theory in the strategic management literature, suggesting 'as evidence of this, Barney's (1991) seminal article which has received more than 1,400 citations according to ISI's social science citation index'(2006: 140). Newbert (2007) says that RBV is 'one of the most widely accepted theoretical perspectives in the strategic management field' and has become 'the dominant theory upon which arguments in academic journals and textbooks alike have been grounded' and that 'much of what we as strategy scholars study, write about, and teach has been greatly influenced by the fundamental arguments of the RBV' (2007: 121).

RBV is underpinned by two key assumptions taken from strategic management theory. First, strategic assets possessed by competing firms may differ (asset heterogeneity) and second, these differences may be long lasting (asset immobility). Therefore if a firm possesses a valuable strategic asset that is not currently possessed by competing firms, it may obtain at least temporary competitive advantage. The second resource-based condition, the condition of asset immobility, becomes important in understanding when a firm's strategic assets will be a source of sustainable competitive advantage. A strategic asset is mobile if firms without it face no cost disadvantage in developing, acquiring and using the strategic asset compared with firms that already possess and use it. In that case, the strategic asset can only be a source of temporary competitive advantage at best. On the other hand, if a firm without a strategic asset does face a cost disadvantage in obtaining, developing and using it (compared with a firm that already possesses it), then the strategic asset can be a source of sustained competitive advantage for the firm that already possesses it (Mata *et al.*, 1995). As we shall discuss, both these conditions have particular significance in the evaluation of IT as a strategic asset, because IT is increasingly perceived to be both homogenous and mobile (the ubiquitous internet being an obvious example).

RBV has been criticised for being a static theory (Priem and Butler, 2001a; 2001b). Priem and Butler point out that the processes through which particular resources provide competitive advantage remain in a 'black box'. However Barney (1991) had acknowledged that the actions necessary to exploit resources must be self-evident and he later came to put more emphasis on implementation and resource exploitation (Barney and Wright, 1998; Barney and Mackey, 2005). Other researchers focused on the use and exploitation of resources rather than their mere possession (Mahoney and Pandian, 1992; Peteraf, 1993; Henderson and Cockburn, 1994). This included research into the process of resource development as core capabilities (Leonard-Barton, 1992); competencies (Reed and DeFillippi, 1990; Fiol, 1991) combinative capabilities (Kogot and Zander, 1992); transformation based competencies (Lado and Wilson, 1994); and organisational competencies (Russo and Fouts, 1997).

Newbert (2007) clearly believes that RBV's transition from static to dynamic theory is complete when he writes 'originally formalised in 1991 as a rather static list of the ingredients for competitive advantage, it has evolved into a dynamic recipe explaining the process by which these ingredients must be utilised to attain this end' (2007: 124). Significantly, he includes in this transition the development of the concept of dynamic capabilities (Teece *et al.*, 1997; Eisenhardt and Martin, 2000) which is based upon earlier work on the development of organisational routines (Nelson and Winter, 1982; Winter, 1987). Thus resources are necessary but not sufficient for competitive advantage, and firms must be able to develop and change their resources to realise their full potential. Again the connections between resource-based theory and Penrose and between resource-based theory and dynamic capabilities are made.

Yet, at the outset Barney (1991: 102) positioned his work within equilibrium when he wrote 'following Lippman and Rumelt (1982) and Rumelt (1984) a competitive advantage is sustained only if continues to exist after efforts to duplicate that advantage have ceased. In this sense, this definition of sustained competitive advantage is an equilibrium definition.' So sustained competitive advantage is not determined by calendar time but by the inability of other firms to copy (and thus compete away) this advantage under normal market conditions (of static equilibrium).

Barney (1991) recognises another source and type of competitive advantage. 'Unanticipated changes in the economic structure of an industry may make what was, at one time, a source of sustained competitive advantage, no longer valuable for the firm, and thus not a source of competitive advantage. These structural revolutions in an industry – called "Schumpeterian Shocks" by several authors (for example, Barney, 1986b; Rumelt and Wensley, 1981) redefine which of a firm's attributes are resources and which are not' (1991: 103). Under these new conditions, some resources may be strengths, others may be weaknesses and still others may be irrelevant. Thus a firm which is enjoying competitive advantage (under conditions of static equilibrium) may have this competitive advantage nullified by Schumpeterian shocks. This is quite different from having the competitive advantage competed away by other firms through duplication and appropriation of its benefits (as under normal market conditions).

Whereas IO economics emphasises asset homogeneity and mobility at industry level, RBV emphasises asset heterogeneity and immobility at firm level. But both are rooted firmly in conditions of static equilibrium. Under IO, competitive advantage is achieved through market power – the exploitation of inefficiencies in market structure. Under RBV, competitive advantage is achieved through (differentiated) firm resources, and not *only* through the exploitation of inefficiencies in market structure.

Amit and Schoemaker (1993) highlight the overlap between and interdependence of IO and RBV. Heterogeneity and immobility of resources would not exist in conditions of perfect competition but rather owe their existence to imperfections within the market. If all firms have equal access to resources (for example, under conditions of perfect competition) then these could not be the source of competitive advantage. The link between IO and RBV is encapsulated in their definition and discussion of strategic industry factors (SIFs): 'when an industry (or product market) is the unit of analysis, one may observe that, at any given time, certain resources and capabilities [SIFs] , which are subject to market failures, have become the prime determinants of economic rents' (1993: 36). Here SIFs are resource based but industry determined. They vary not only between firms but between industries. A firm's resources are strategic only in the context of the industry in which they are held and deployed (and relative to the resources of other firms) so that 'the applicability of the firm's bundle of resources and capabilities to a particular industry setting (i.e. the overlap with the set of strategic industry factors) will determine available rents' (ibid.: 39).

Amit and Schoemaker (1993) refer to uncertainty in strategic decision making (in and out of equilibrium) but (again) are mostly concerned with the situation pertaining at equilibrium. So that 'the supposition is that even in equilibrium, firms may differ in terms of the resources and capabilities they control, and that such asymmetric firms may co-exist until some exogenous change or Schumpeterian shock occurs'. They also state 'the assumption that heterogeneous firms controlling resources that are not perfectly mobile (i.e. that cannot be easily, bought, sold or imitated) is essential to the existence of such equilibrium' (ibid.: 37–38).

Here, as in Barney (1991), Schumpeter is introduced almost as an afterthought, as an exogenous change that disrupts equilibrium (which is the context for their strategising).[5] There is no discussion of innovation or endogenous change or economic development, or of the implications of this for management theory and practice. When discussing RBV, Amit and Schoemaker rightly say that 'the exclusive focus on equilibrium and structural dimensions is absent (compared to industrial analysis)' but incorrectly say that (in RBV) 'disequilibrium and process dynamics loom primary' (1993: 42). This latter statement is not borne out by their own treatment of resource-based theory, nor by that of Barney.

Amit and Schoemaker (1993) further distinguish between the accumulation of capabilities which is dynamic and the deployment of capabilities which is static. There is a trade-off in developing capabilities under equilibrium and their use in periods of disequilibrium – the more specialised the asset, the less valuable it will be when the circumstances for which it has been developed change. Amit later acknowledged the difficulty of applying RBV in volatile markets, such as in virtual markets, where there is a high degree of mobility of information-based strategic assets (Amit and Zott, 2001). In virtual markets strategic assets are hard to sustain, and the application of RBV in internet research is problematical. This suggests both the limitations of RBV and avenues for its extension.

A major criticism of RBV arises from its perceived usage of insufficient definitions (Foss, 1997; 2005; Priem and Butler, 2001a; 2001b). Foss believes that the inconsistent use of definitions for resources, capabilities and dynamic capabilities in different publications is confusing, and leads to the risk of tautology. Priem and Butler contend that Barney's (1991) main assertions are true by definition and therefore not falsifiable (according to Popper's (1959) theory). They argue that 'the underlying problem in the statement that valuable and rare organisational resources can be a source of competitive advantage (Barney, 1991: 107) is that competitive advantage is defined in terms of value and rarity, and the resource characteristics argued to lead to competitive advantage are value and rarity. Instead, the characteristics and outcomes must be conceptualised independently to produce a synthetic statement' (Priem and Butler, 2001b: 28).

Porter (1991: 108) had already identified this problem when he wrote 'at its worst, the resource based view is circular. Successful firms are successful because they have unique resources. They should nurture these resources to be successful. But what is a unique resource? What makes it valuable?' Priem and Butler suggest resolving the tautology by using Schoemaker's definition of competitive advantage ('systematically creating above average returns': Schoemaker, 1990: 1179) that also includes factors that are external to the firm. Similarly,

Peteraf (1993) and Foss (2005) advocate the use of economic rents as dependent variables in resource-based research because they are 'unambiguously defined and consistently used in the literature' (Foss, 2005: 300). Barney (2001a: 48) has partially replied to these criticisms by accepting that both definitions of competitive advantage (financial and non-financial) would be feasible but that researchers should 'specify exactly what it is they are trying to explain: above-average industry profits (as in Priem and Butler), a firm improving its efficiency and effectiveness in ways that competing firms are not ... or economic rents'.

Porter (1991) also (and perhaps unsurprisingly) criticises RBV for being introspective, and in particular, for ignoring the environment and the industry within which the company operates. He argues that the resource-based view and the market-based view are not mutually exclusive; rather they complement each other. This is a view increasingly held by researchers in strategic management (Barney, 2001b; Collis and Montgomery, 1995; Mahoney, 1995; Makadok, 2001). The use of the two approaches separately across a number of different research studies has obvious appeal in developing a holistic picture of firm performance, but applying both approaches within the same research study can be problematical, not least because of the potential conflict between two sets of ontologies, goals and methods. Moreover, combining RBV and IO approaches does not address significant shortcomings in RBV.

A final criticism of RBV is that, although there have been many individual tests of specific hypotheses, there have been very few summary reviews of the results of these tests (Newbert, 2007, found only one such review: that of Barney and Arikan, 2001). Overall Barney and Arikan (2001) report a high degree of support for RBV but Newbert (2007) argues that this is misleading because (a) Barney and Arikan looked only for tests that were counter to RBV and did not include those that merely were inconsistent or inclusive, and (b) their study was subject to selection bias because it was limited to the field with which they are familiar. Newbert (2007: 122) claims to have carried out 'the first systematic assessment of RBV's level of empirical support'. He found that RBV has received only modest support overall and that the level of support varies considerably with the independent variable and theoretical approach employed. One finding is that most attention has been paid to the study of resources, but capabilities and competencies have been far more significant in explaining competitive advantage. This suggests again that the choice of independent variable (as well as the choice of the dependent variable) is important to the outcomes of the study.

The further development of RBV is largely motivated by criticisms and limitations of the original concept. Prahalad and Hamel (1990) made a significant contribution to the development of RBV through their concept of core competencies. Subsequently, partially in response to criticism that RBV did not explain how and why certain firms have competitive advantage in situations of rapid and unpredictable changing markets, Hamel and Valikangas (2003) developed the concept of organisational resilience. The resilience concept combines the core competencies concept (Prahalad and Hamel, 1990) and the dynamic capabilities framework (Teece *et al.*, 1997). Resilience is defined as 'the capacity for continuous reconstruction' (Hamel and Valikangas, 2003: 55) and is the ability to dynamically invent or re-invent business models and strategies as circumstances change. However, the concept of resilience has also been criticised. Core competencies can become competency traps (Levitt and March, 1988) or core rigidities (Leonard-Barton, 1992). We shall return to the concept of resilience in Chapter 6, as an illustration of the need to implement the right balance of management and leadership in order to achieve sustainable competitive advantage.

Another development of the RBV can be found in the knowledge-based view of the firm (Grant, 1996; 1997). In this perspective, knowledge is the most important of the firm's resources (indeed the firm is conceptualised as an institution for integrating knowledge) and interest is focused on the coordination mechanisms through which firms integrate specialist knowledge for their members. Teece *et al.* (1997) extended Grant's work on the coordination and integration of knowledge to other assets, such as technology. They also included additional capabilities, for example the reconfiguration of resources. Eisenhardt and Martin (2000) further enhanced this line of research by including other capabilities, such as exit routines that jettison resources. These developments, and others in response to the limitations of RBV, led to the development of the concept of dynamic capabilities.

Dynamic capabilities

Both Mahoney (1995) and Makadok (2001) quote Williamson (1991) who observed that 'the leading efficiency approaches to business strategy are the resource-based and the dynamic capabilities approach … it is not obvious to me how these two literatures will play out – either individually or in combination. Plainly they deal with core issues.

Possibly they will be joined' (1991: 76). Mahoney believes that 'the two approaches naturally blend into each other' (1995: 91) and Makadok concludes that 'the two rent creating mechanisms are certainly not mutually exclusive, and it is likely that firms generally use both of them' and that they 'are complementary in some circumstances but substitutes in others' (2001: 387).

Penrose was concerned with limitations on growth (in static equilibrium) and with the limitations of focusing only on existing resources and capabilities. She therefore stressed, as did Schumpeter, the need to innovate during periods of disequilibrium. This was different from innovation during periods of equilibrium. Penrose wrote about the 'normal' use of resources and capabilities and the use of these in abnormal circumstances. She is claimed (with some justification) as an advocate for both resource-based theory and dynamic capabilities but her primary advocacy is for DC because she is concerned with a theory of the growth of the firm, and economic growth – as defined by Schumpeter – is a function of innovation during periods of disequilibrium. Unfortunately, as we have seen in the previous chapter, it is her contribution to RBV through her focus on resources and capabilities that is most remembered, and she is used to justify the development of Ricardian rents and market position.

It is clear that Levitas and Ndofor (2006) see dynamic capabilities as an extension of RBV when they accuse Gibbert (2006) of 'falling prey to a common trap' in believing that Barney (1991) represented 'the current and most advanced state of RBV thinking' and therefore ignoring 'more recent research in the RBV that focuses on the dynamic aspects of capabilities' (Levitas and Ndofor, 2006: 140). They cite the history of IBM's transformations from a punch card manufacturer, to a manufacturer of tabulators, time clocks and typewriters, to a mainframe manufacturer, to a PC company, to a services company, as evidence of 'the ability to change and adapt resources and/or capabilities to maintain superiority'. In doing so, they suggest a transition from Ricardian to Schumpeterian rents, and an evolution from resource-based theory to dynamic capabilities.

Teece and his co-authors (1997) developed the dynamic capabilities framework which analyses the sources and methods of wealth creation and capture by firms operating in environments of rapid technological change. In doing so they clearly envisage Schumpeterian (as opposed to Ricardian or monopoly) rents. They claim that their framework

> suggests that private wealth creation in regimes of rapid technological change depends in large measure on holding internal

technological, organisational, and managerial processes inside the firm. In short, identifying new opportunities and organising effectively and efficiently to embrace them are generally more fundamental to private wealth creation than is strategising, if by strategising one means engaging in business conduct that keeps competitors off balance, raises rival's costs, and excludes new entrants.

(1997: 509)

They also establish the interdependence of resource-based theory and IO analysis. Under the competitive forces approach, a firm picks an asset on which to compete but unless the firm has superior information on that asset then it will only generate normal returns from its acquisition, and hence that asset cannot be a source of competitive advantage. So differential resources (knowledge) are necessary to a successful IO strategy, and market imperfections are necessary to the development (and protection) of firm-specific assets. The real difference between the two approaches is that under IO the firm chooses the market in which to compete before the assets it will use to compete, whereas, under RBV the firms choose the assets and then the market.

Teece and his co-authors also distinguish between monopoly rents and Ricardian rents. Whereas monopoly rents result from strategies that secure superior product/market positioning (through raising barriers to entry, or raising prices, for example), Ricardian rents are the result of the accumulation and deployment of firm specific resources and therefore 'upstream of product market positioning' (Teece *et al.*, 1997: 513). Whereas monopoly rents are the concern of IO, structure-conduct-performance (SCP) and other industry analysis approaches (Mason, 1939; Bain, 1968; Porter, 1980), Ricardian rents are the concern of resource-based theory (Penrose, 1959; Barney, 1991). Moreover, although there is overlap (as indicated above), the importance of product market positioning in determining firm performance is often overplayed because it is difficult to define markets, strategies based upon particular product market positions are fragile during periods of rapid technological change, and 'the link between market share and innovation has long been broken, if it ever existed' (Teece *et al.*, 1997: 522).

Here, Penrose is cited as an antecedent of RBV and of dynamic capabilities because of the shared notion that 'competitive advantage requires both the exploitation of existing internal and external firm specific capabilities, and developing new ones' (Teece *et al.*, 1997: 515). But, as we have seen, dynamic capabilities are firmly based on

Schumpeterian theory and need no introduction through Penrose and resource-based theory.

Similar to RBV, the concept of dynamic capabilities has been criticised as being vague and tautological (Mosakowski and McKelvey, 1997; Williamson, 1991; and Priem and Butler, 2001b), lacking empirical grounding (Williamson, 1991; Priem and Butler, 2001b) and unlikely to deliver sustained competitive advantage in dynamic markets (D'Aveni, 1994). Eisenhardt and Martin (2000) in a direct response to these criticisms (particularly the last one) develop and extend the concept.

They discuss the impact of the market environment on dynamic capabilities and distinguish between those developed and used in moderately dynamic markets and those developed and used in high-velocity markets. Moderately dynamic markets are characterised by a stable industry structure, defined boundaries, clear business models, identifiable players and linear and predictable change. Here dynamic capabilities take the form of routines, i.e. detailed, analytical, stable processes with predictable outcomes. High-velocity markets, in contrast, are characterised by an ambiguous industry structure, blurred boundaries, fluid business models, ambiguous and shifting players, and non-linear and unpredictable change. Here dynamic capabilities are simple, highly experimental and fragile processes with unpredictable outcomes.

Eisenhardt and Martin take dynamic capabilities as a necessary extension of RBV, because RBV does not work in volatile markets. But they also carry forward the notion of dualism of equilibrium and disequilibrium. In moderately dynamic markets where the environment is static, dynamic capabilities take the form of routines. In high-velocity markets, characterised by disequilibrium, dynamic capabilities take the form of strategic improvisations. Both are scenarios of organisational strategising but their focus is on what happens in volatile markets.

In volatile (or high-velocity) markets, dynamic capabilities are simple, experimental routines that rely on newly created knowledge specific to the situation. But they are also ambiguous (as in moderately dynamic markets, but here it is because of their simplicity, not their complexity). So, 'the extensive, experiential activity of effective dynamic capabilities in high velocity markets obscures the fundamental commonalities that drive the effectiveness of the capability' and 'it is difficult to isolate causality from the extensive, but unimportant idiosyncratic details'. Such causal ambiguity makes evaluation of dynamic capabilities difficult because 'sometimes even managers

themselves do not know why their dynamic capabilities are successful'
(Eisenhardt and Martin, 2000: 1114).

Lockett and Thompson (2001) rationalise causal ambiguity by
recourse to economic theory. They suggest that Barney's (1991) concept
of causal ambiguity is linked to the position of the Austrian School that
the sources of business success are barely observable. An important
difference, however, is that whereas in RBV ambiguity is rooted in the
nature of the historical path dependency and complexity, in the Austrian
School the ambiguity is rooted in the nature of perception itself. Further,
'it is also a central part of the Austrian school view that entrepreneurs
can and do make mistakes. Thus, firm evolution does not necessarily
follow an optimal trajectory' (2001: 745) and, because of historical path
dependency, poor choices in the past can lead to poor choices in the
future.

They speculate further on 'some potentially useful insights into
RBV' afforded by Austrian economics. First because the Austrian
School is concerned with what happens at disequilibrium, differences in
firm performance are not necessarily associated with market power, and
therefore there is no need for the existence of limits to market
competition in order to create a position of competitive advantage.
Second, the importance of entrepreneurial discovery in Austrian
economics links RBV with entrepreneurship research.

It is clear that Lockett and Thompson (2001) unequivocally associate
RBV with static equilibrium when they say 'it is perhaps inevitable that
the RBV, given its convenience as a tool for understanding observed
competitive advantage, is widely (if implicitly) presented as a static
theory. That is, the possession of some difficult to replicate firm specific
advantage allows the firm to sustain rents in the face of competition
from less fortunate rivals' (2001: 744). This reflects the dominance of
traditional IO thinking; but RBV can also be viewed as a dynamic or
evolutionary theory 'in which each firm's resource bundle is evolving
along its own unique trajectory as a consequence of the firm's unique
history' (ibid.: 744). This has encouraged a shift in emphasis from
external to internal advantages but (because of the continued dominance
of IO thinking) has 'led to little change in methods' (ibid.: 755).

In a discussion that resonates with that surrounding the concept of
creative destruction (namely, whether it is revolutionary or evolutionary
in nature) Lockett and Thompson further explore the concept of
dynamic capabilities. If dynamic capabilities are defined as the firm's
ability to update and improve the sources of its own competitive
advantage (Teece *et al.*, 1997) then this itself is a resource based on past
experience and will be heavily path dependent. Therefore dynamic

capabilities may be better able to explain incremental rather than radical change. The question then becomes what explains radical change? They do not elaborate but hint at exogenous change when they say 'there will usually be some more proximate cause for radical change to enter the organisation's agenda' (Lockett and Thompson 2001: 745). However, as noted in the previous chapter in relation to the development of Schumpeter's theory, this suggests admitting a non-economic answer to an economic problem.

Makadok (2001) seeks a synthesis of resource-based and dynamic capability views on rent creation. Whereas for those who take the Ricardian perspective (codified into the RBV) resource picking is the main source of economic rent, for those who take the Schumperterian perspective (codified into the dynamic capability view) capability building is the main source of economic rent. The first approach necessarily takes place ex ante and the second approach *ex post*.[6] However, the relationship between resources and capabilities is complex and simple causality cannot be assumed. So, for example, the act of resource picking may itself be regarded as a capability, one that is developed more as it is exercised more. Thus when a firm is considering the acquisition of a resource 'the first type of advantage to be considered is a capability advantage' (2001: 392).[7]

The implications for managers of one important difference between resources and capabilities are clear enough. Whereas resources are generic (and can be bought and therefore managers require expertise in acquisitions), capabilities are embedded and firm specific and must be built. Therefore 'the manager's role may be more nearly analogous to an architect than to a stock-picker trying to beat the market' (Makadok 2001: 389). He concludes that the distinction (between the resource picking and capability mechanisms) 'cuts directly to the core of the rent creation process' (ibid.: 389). If resource picking is the primary mechanism for creating rents, then managers make their contribution largely through forming expectations about the value to their company of acquiring particular resources. In such circumstances strategy should focus on information and cognition, that is, on the information collected to inform strategy formulation and the cognitive processes used for filtering that information when choosing which resources to acquire and when forming expectations of the value of those resources to the firm. On the other hand, if capability building is the primary mechanism for creating rents, then managers make their contribution largely through designing and constructing capabilities internally (ibid.: 389–390).

Sometimes resource picking will take precedence over capability building and sometimes not. It very much depends upon the circumstances of the firm. Sometimes the two mechanisms will complement one another, and sometimes they will be substitutes for each other. Makadok notes: 'it seems likely that firms would generally use some combination of both mechanisms, that the two mechanisms do not act independently of each other, and that their relative importance in generating economic rents would be a function of the firm's internal and external circumstances' (2001: 391). This suggests that resource picking will be more appropriate during periods of static equilibrium and capabilities will be more appropriate during periods of disequilibrium.

Both Teece *et al.* (1997) and Eisenhardt and Martin (2000) examine the development of dynamic capabilities, identifying three key stages – building, integrating and re-configuring assets. In the next chapter (Chapter 4) we highlight the relationship between dynamic capabilities and firm performance (measured as financial performance) using statistical analysis of small businesses. In the following chapter (Chapter 5) we examine empirically the development of dynamic capabilities (at each of the three stages – building, integrating and re-configuring assets) by owner-managers in small IT companies, using interpretative analysis.

IT as a strategic asset

Where does all this leave IT? So far in this chapter we have sought to provide a context for the study of IT and competitive advantage through a discussion of the strategic management literature. We have introduced resource-based theory and dynamic capabilities. We have discussed the relationship between these theories and economic theory, specifically, the economic theory of Joseph Schumpeter. We have noted a discordance between Schumpeter's theory (and Penrose's application of it to the firm) and much of the literature on the provenance and contribution of the RBV. This discordance has been, and continues to be, manifested in the 'Schumpeterian hypothesis'. In this and in the previous chapter, we have pointed out the misinterpretation of Schumpeter's writings on innovation and economic growth contained within the Schumpeterian hypothesis, and sought, through careful unravelling of economic and management theories, to establish a solid foundation upon which strategic assets can be studied and understood.

Lack of clarity in the study of strategic assets has led to difficulties for researchers and practitioners. What is meant by competitive advantage? What is a strategic asset? What is the difference between resources and capabilities? What is the difference between a static and a dynamic capability? Can a capability be both static (in implementation) and dynamic (in development)? Added to these questions, there is an emerging consensus that, because of the complex nature of organisational and human economic and social activity, we may never know exactly what is going on, and the relationships between assets and their causalities will always remain something of a mystery.

We now turn to examine IT as a strategic asset. In doing so, we seek to focus on the unique characteristics of IT as a strategic asset but accept that this is not possible unless we also consider how IT interacts with other strategic assets. The remainder of this chapter reviews the general literature on the relationship between IT and competitive advantage. The next chapter is focused upon empirical studies of IT's direct and indirect impact on firm performance. The resource-based view was originally developed in strategic management research, but has also been deployed in other research areas, for example in information technology (IT) and information systems (IS) research. Wade and Hulland (2004) suggest that the RBV can be used as a framework to evaluate the value of strategic IS assets and for comparing IS assets with non-IS assets.

Many of the early resource-based studies in IS research identified and defined strategic IS assets. Ross *et al.* (1996) identified the following three IT assets: human assets (for example, problem solving orientation, business understanding and technical skills), technology assets (for example, physical IT assets, technical platforms and databases) and relationship assets (for example, partnerships with other divisions, client relationships and shared risks and responsibility). Feeny and Willcocks (1998) identified nine core IS capabilities: IS/IT governance, business systems thinking, relationship building, designing technical architecture, making technology work, informed buying, contract facilitation, contract monitoring and vendor development. Bharadwaj (2000) defined IT infrastructure, human IT resources and IT enabled intangibles as IT resources.

Bharadwaj (2001) argued that the capability to deploy these IT resources synergistically with other strategic assets can lead to competitive advantage. She found out that firms with high IT capability tended to outperform a control sample of firms on a variety of profit and cost-based performance measures. Santhanam and Hartono (2003) extended this study with a more sophisticated methodology and came to very similar results. Zhang and Lado (2001) argued that the potential contributions of IS to competitive advantage can be understood in terms of their impact on the development and utilisation of distinctive organisational competences (input-based competences, transformation-based competences and output-based competences). Tippins and Sohi (2003) divided IT assets into IT knowledge, IT operations and IT objects and showed that IT affects organisational learning, which is related to firm performance. Clearly IT is more than a commodity.

The 'productivity paradox' (Brynjolfsson and Hitt, 2000; Willcocks and Lester, 1996) implies that the relationship of IT assets to firm performance is still unclear and controversial.[8] Whereas early case studies suggested a direct relationship between IT and firm performance (Copeland and McKenney, 1988; Short and Venkatraman, 1992), more recent research has frequently been inconclusive (Kettinger *et al.*, 1994; Powell and Dent-Micallef, 1997). Wade and Hulland (2004) summarised the research on the relationship of IT to firm performance in a table. See Table 3.1.

More recent research has still not uncovered the relationship between IT and performance: Some studies suggest a direct and positive relationship (Duh *et al.*, 2006; Theodorou and Florou, 2006; Merono-Cerdan and Soto-Acousta, 2007), others find no direct relationship, but an indirect or contingent effect (Ruiz-Mercader *et al.*, 2006; Neirotti and Paolucci, 2007). Still others find no effect at all (Martinsons and Leung, 2002), or conclude that the relationship is inconclusive or even elusive (Chen, 2000).

One of the first papers that was embedded in resource-based theory and discussed the role of IT was written by Clemons and Row in 1991. They argued that IT assets *per se* cannot create sustainable competitive advantage. This has been supported by further IT research and cumulatively has provided a perspective known as the 'strategic necessity hypothesis' to which most IT researchers now adhere (for example, see Clemons and Kimbrough, 1986; Clemons and Row, 1991; Kettinger *et al.*, 1994; Porter, 2001). The strategic necessity hypothesis implies that companies that do not control basic IT assets may create competitive disadvantages. But basic IT assets (such as hardware, software, and related processes) can be copied relatively easily, and thus cannot be a source of sustainable competitive advantage. However, IT assets in the form of firm-specific capabilities and competencies such as knowledge, skills and experiences, cannot be easily copied and therefore offer the prospect of sustainable competitive advantage. Porter (2001) argued that though the ubiquitous internet cannot alone confer competitive advantage it may be used as part of a resource bundle to achieve that outcome.

Clemons and Row (1991: 275) argued that information systems can 'radically change cost structures, relative bargaining power, or the basis of competition to an extent where most competitors are compelled to imitate them'. However, because competitors often imitate them or respond before customers change their behaviour, these systems seldom

Table 3.1 Effect of IS on firm performance*

Outcome effect	Relevant studies
Direct and positive Information technology has a direct and positive effect on competitive advantage or performance	Banker and Kauffman (1991); Bharadwaj (2000); Clemons and Weber (1990); Floyd and Woolridge (1990); Jelassi and Figon (1994); Mahmood (1993); Mahmood and Mann (1993); Mahmood and Soon (1991); Roberts *et al.* (1990); Silverman (1999); Tavakolian (1989); Tyran *et al.* (1992); Yoo and Choi (1990)
Direct and negative Information technology has a negative effect on competitive advantage or performance	Warner (1987)
No effect Information technology has no impact on competitive advantage or performance	Sager (1988); Venkatraman and Zaheer (1990)
Contingent effect The effect of information technology on competitive advantage or performance depends on other constructs	Banker and Kauffman (1988); Carrol and Larkin (1992); Clemons and Row (1988); Clemons and Row (1991); Copeland and McKenney (1988); Feeny and Ives (1990); Henderson and Sifonis (1988); Holland *et al.* (1992); Johnston and Carrico (1988); Kettinger et al. (1994); Kettinger *et al.* (1995); King *et al.* (1989); Lederer and Sethi (1988); Li and Ye (1999); Lindsey *et al.* (1990); Mann *et al.* (1991); Neo (1988); Powell and Dent-Micallef (1997); Reich and Benbasat (1996); Schwarzer (1995)

*Note: IT refers to the use of IT resources or IT capability, and not the mere possession of those resources. For example, Bharadwaj (2000) demonstrated a link between IT capability and superior firm performance. Also, the same study can find evidence to support different relationships. So for example, Kettinger *et al.* (1994) and Powell and Dent-Micallef (1997) both found that IT had a negative direct impact on firm performance but a positive indirect impact on firm performance. In this table such studies are accredited on the basis of their substantive findings.

Source: From Wade and Hulland, 2004.

confer competitive advantage. It could even be that 'the copying firm often enjoys the advantages of newer and better technology, learns from the experience of the innovator, and thus can offer comparable services at lower costs'. Indeed, as we have suggested earlier, the imitating firm may be at a competitive advantage over the innovating firm precisely because it is better able to develop the capabilities needed to exploit the benefits of the new technology.

Amit and Zott (2001) have reviewed the application of strategic management theories to virtual markets, which they describe as 'settings in which business transactions are conducted via open networks that are based on the fixed and wireless internet infrastructure (2001: 495). They acknowledge the impact of the internet on a firm's value chain. The internet, for example, can add value to sales and fulfilment services, as happened when Amazon decided to build its own warehouses in order to increase the speed and reliability of the delivery of its products. The internet can also change the roles and relationships of between key stakeholders, such as customers, partners and suppliers. However, Amit and Zott suggest that the value chain analysis (Porter, 1985; 2001) may be too simplistic for virtual markets, because of the way in which the internet enables new combinations of information, physical products and services, new and innovative configurations of transactions, and new integration and re-configuration of strategic assets.

Amit and Zott (2001) suggest that the internet broadens the notion of innovation because it may change firm and industry boundaries and may enable new exchange mechanisms and new forms of collaborations between firms. They believe that although 'innovation is certainly a major driving force in the development of new and established markets, it may not be the only source of value creation in virtual markets' (2001: 497). Similarly, although the internet may enhance the importance of strategic networks (e.g. strategic alliances, joint ventures, and long-term buyer–supplier relationships), the novel ways of transacting by the internet are not fully covered by network theory. Finally, they point out that although the internet can reduce transaction costs and may enable transactions between previously unconnected parties, transaction cost economics with its focus on costs and efficiency may be insufficient for analysing competitive advantage in virtual environments. They conclude that the resource-based view is the most appropriate method to analyse the strategic impact of the internet.

Wade and Hulland's (2004) review of the literature indicates the number of studies on the impact of IT on firm performance but there is little agreement on the strategic value of IT, even among subsequent studies. This has been blamed on differences in usage of data and measurements (Brynjolfsson, 1993), and differences in sample size, industry type, and choice of dependent variable, but as Oh and Pinsonneault (2007) make clear, another, and perhaps more important, reason is the use of different research frameworks. They compare and contrast 'two perspectives [that] have been predominantly used as the conceptual basis to study strategic information technologies' (2007: 240). These are the resource-centred view and the contingency-based view (Tosi and Slocum, 1984; Fry and Smith, 1987). Their article is a timely reminder that although RBV is the most popular theoretical approach to the study of IT, it is not the only one, and not necessarily the best.

In a study of 110 CEOs and CIOs of small manufacturing firms, Oh and Pinsonneault (2007) conclude that the resource-centred approach is better at predicting the ability of IT to impact firm revenue and profitability, but the contingency-based approach is better at explaining the impact of cost-related IT applications on firm performance. So, 'IT alignment with a cost reduction strategy generates more immediate and tangible benefits for firms than IT-strategy alignment that aims to facilitate revenue growth'. Also, and perhaps less surprisingly, 'extracting benefits from strategic IS resources designed to help firms grow is more difficult than extracting benefits from operational IS resources developed to cut costs' (2007: 259).

It is important to remember at this point that the contingency-based approach to which Oh and Pinsonneault refer is specifically concerned with the alignment of IT and business strategy. This is quite different from general contingency approaches (such as those included in the Wade and Hulland review of IS research studies) that study IT's indirect impact on firm performance, considering IT's interaction or complementarity with a range of other resources. Yet even in the much narrower interpretation to which Oh and Pinsonneault refer, there is little consensus.

We may expect IT assets used in support of business strategy to have a greater impact on firm performance than IT assets not used for this purpose. Some studies have shown this, for example Sambamurthy and Zmud, 1992, Dierickx and Cool 1989; but others have not, or are inconclusive. Oh and Pinsonneault attribute this to the same set of problems that are found in RBV research – different studies, different approaches, and different measures of organisational performance. Clearly more research of greater clarity and consistency is required in both research streams before the conundrum that is IT and competitive advantage can be better understood and explained.

Conclusion

Based upon the review of the strategic management literature in this chapter, and that of underlying economic theories in the previous chapter, we can now offer some observations on the nature of the relationship between IT and competitive advantage.

Both Wade and Hulland (2004) and Oh and Pinsonneault (2007) highlight the extent to which the research community differs in its understanding of this relationship. Some studies show that IT has a direct and positive impact on competitive advantage, but many others do not – the impact may be indirect; there may be no impact at all (either direct or indirect), the impact (direct or indirect) may be negative, or we simply can not tell what that impact (direct or indirect, positive or negative) may be.

The application of RBV to the study of IT and competitive advantage would appear to suggest that IT cannot be the source of competitive advantage. IT is neither heterogeneous nor immobile, and as an asset that is both readily available and easily imitated it would appear to offer no prospects for long-term or sustained competitive advantage. Yet IT as a strategic asset is more than hardware, software, operations and processes. Strategic IT is built on knowledge (managerial and technical), firm-specific skills, experiences and historical path dependencies. Hence, IT is not homogeneous and mobile but heterogeneous and immobile. IT *may* be a source of sustained competitive advantage, but not directly.

Most researchers no longer believe that IT can impact competitive advantage directly (studies that claimed to find a direct relationship have long since been superseded by studies claiming only a contingency effect). However, evidence of indirect impacts is still controversial because it has proven so difficult to unravel resource bundles of causal ambiguity. Claims that IT is a complementary strategic asset or a strategic enabler of other assets are often barely more credible than claims that IT *per se* is a strategic asset. Precisely because the evidence is frequently inconclusive, it is tempting to claim that IT has no strategic importance at all. There is a danger that IT may be discounted as a strategic asset as much by research fragmentation as by technology commoditisation.

Newbert (2007) has pointed out a general problem in RBV research which applies also to IT research. Despite increased acceptance of the importance of capabilities to firm performance, many researchers still measure only resources. Resources are easier to measure than capabilities, not only because they are less complex but because resource measures are more readily derived from secondary data. For example, whereas human resources can be measured by the number and type of staff employed, human resources capability has been operationalized as 18 HR policies (Hatch and Dyer, 2004). Similarly, IT resources can be measured as the number, type and cost of resources available, including IT human resources, but IT capability must be measured across a much broader spectrum, including ability to manage IT infrastructure, to formulate and maintain internal and external strategic networks and alliances, and so on. All of these measures are observable only through primary research and it is perhaps little wonder that much IT research, like much RBV research in general, uses secondary resource data.[9]

Adding to this equivocation and reluctance in the measurement of independent variables, researchers frequently use different definitions and measures of the dependent variable of competitive advantage. In Chapter 1 we defined competitive advantage as economic rents. This definition has the advantage (as Foss (2005) has pointed out) of being coherent both intrinsically (in terms of the logic of economic systems) and extrinsically (in terms of its application in different research settings). However, we also acknowledged that economic rents are hard to measure and that for practicable purposes in the study of organisational performance, surrogate measures are required. Of the many that are available, most researchers take the expedient of measuring profits. But this too has many different definitions.

4   IT and the creation of Ricardian rents

Introduction

In the previous chapter we identified two different rent-creating mechanisms within the resource-based logic. Under the Ricardian perspective (as codified in the resource-based view) resource picking is the main source of economic rents. Under the Schumpeterian perspective (as codified in the dynamic capability view) capability building is the main source of economic rent. For Makadok (2001: 389) this distinction 'cuts directly to the core of the rent creation process'.

Under the RBV if a strategic assets fulfils the following requirements it can be a source of Ricardian rents: (1) strategic assets differ between competing firms (asset heterogeneity) and (2) these differences are long lasting (asset immobility). We suggest that those IT assets that are used by several competing firms cannot be sources of competitive advantage because the assertion of asset heterogeneity is not met. This means that those IT assets that can easily be purchased, (for example, standardised hardware, standardised software, common IT knowledge and internet access), cannot be a source of competitive advantage and Ricardian rents. Furthermore, IT could only be a source of sustainable competitive advantage if firms without IT assets are at competitive disadvantage in acquiring, developing and using IT assets (asset immobility).

We conclude that IT assets that are freely available cannot create sustained competitive advantage but that IT may enable competitive advantage through its interaction with other strategic assets. In particular, IT can be complementary. 'Complementarity represents an enhancement of resource value, and arises when a resource produces greater returns in the presence of another resource than it does alone' (Powell and Dent-Micallef, 1997: 379). Under the resource-based view, a complementary interaction typically enhances the value for both (or all) strategic assets, although the causality may be ambiguous (Barney, 1991).

In this chapter we investigate empirically IT's potential for creating Ricardian rents, and in Chapter 5 we investigate IT's potential for creating Schumpeterian rents in a discussion of the development of dynamic capabilities. Then, in Chapter 6, we compare and contrast these two rent-creation mechanisms and relate these to the management of IT.

This chapter proceeds as follows. First, we introduce the conceptual framework used to investigate the direct and indirect impact of IT on firm performance. This is an adaptation of Powell and Dent-Micallef's (1997) study of large firms. We explain why and how their framework was modified to make it more appropriate to the study of small firms. We set out the relationships (and associated hypotheses) to be empirically tested. These relate specifically to the proposed direct impact of IT on financial performance but also include, by way of comparison, the impact of business resources and dynamic capabilities on financial performance. We then consider the indirect impact of IT on firm performance, setting out proposed relationships and associated hypotheses concerning the complementarity of IT assets to dynamic capabilities and business resources, and the complementarity of the internet to dynamic capabilities, business resources and IT assets. Then we introduce our research study, explaining the sample and measures used, and the method of data analysis. Our results are then presented, conclusions drawn and wider implications discussed.

Research framework and hypotheses

Whereas the resource-based view of the firm has been applied extensively within strategic management research, research on strategic assets in the context of IT and the internet is still rare (see Melville *et al.*, 2004 for a review). Moreover, the resource-based view appears to be especially useful for examining performance differentials among small firms. It has already been suggested that small companies' problems in deploying IT and the internet arise from a lack of strategic assets (Kleindl, 2000; Saban and Rau, 2005), including financial resources (Foong, 1999), IT resources (Igbaria *et al.*, 1998), or lack of owner-managers' technological expertise (Palvia and Palvia, 1999). It has also been suggested that companies seeking to expand into virtual markets need to develop additional strategic assets (Daniel and Wilson, 2003). We therefore employ the RBV to examine the impact of IT on firm performance. The key research questions for this chapter are:

- Does IT directly impact firm performance?
- Does IT indirectly impact firm performance (as a complementary asset)?
- Does the internet indirectly impact firm performance (as a complementary asset)?

Based on the work of Walton (1989) and Keen (1993), Powell and Dent-Micallef (1997) developed a theoretical framework for analysing the relationship of business resources, human resources and IT resources with IT performance and with financial performance. Walton (1989) and Benjamin and Levinson (1993) divided strategic assets into organisational, business and technological assets. Keen (1993) preferred human, business and technology assets. He believed that IT can be used to leverage human resources and business resources and thus create competitive advantage. In our research we modified the Powell and Dent-Micallef (1997) framework as follows.

First, whereas Powell and Dent-Micallef (1997) used human resources as an independent variable, we used the newer concept of dynamic capabilities. Powell and Dent-Micallef's measures were especially designed for large enterprises with human resources departments and cross-sectional teams.[1] These measures are inappropriate for small companies which perform activities with less expertise because they do not have functional specialists (Verhees and Meulenberg, 2004) and whose capabilities are mainly determined by the owner-manager (Jones, 2004). Compared with the construct of human resources, the dynamic capabilities concept is more appropriate for small firms because it evaluates skills at an organisational rather than at a departmental level and it emphasises flexibility which is a typical strength of small firms (Dean *et al.*, 1998). In addition, the wording of some questions was changed in order to make them applicable to small companies in different industries rather than to large retailers only. The questionnaire is given as Appendix A.4.1.

Second, the Powell and Dent-Micallef study measured only technology resources (computer hardware, software and linkages). In our research these were complemented by Tippins and Sohi's (2003) conceptualisation of IT knowledge (the extent to which a firm possesses a body of technical knowledge about objects such as computer-based systems), IT operations (the extent to which a firm utilises IT to manage market and customer information) and IT objects (computer-based hardware, software and support personnel).

The modified Powell and Dent-Micallef framework is presented as Figure 4.1. It comprises the independent variables IT assets, business resources and dynamic capabilities and the dependent variable financial performance.

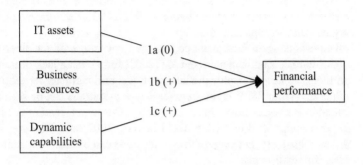

Figure 4.1 The hypothesised relationships between strategic assets and financial performance

In the previous chapter we pointed out that research on the relationship of IT assets to financial performance is frequently inconclusive and that most studies fail to prove IT's direct performance relationships. However, although IT assets may not be directly related to financial performance there may be a contingent effect because IT assets may be complementary to other strategic assets (Clemons and Row, 1991; Powell and Dent-Micallef, 1997). In our research the direct and indirect relationships between IT assets and financial performance were evaluated. It was not expected that IT assets would be directly related to financial performance and therefore we began with a null hypothesis:

Hypothesis 1a: IT assets *do not* explain significant financial performance variance among small firms.

Business resources

Following Powell and Dent-Micallef's (1997) work, business resources were divided into a set of sub-categories: relationships with customers and suppliers; external-driven e-business; benchmarking; strategic use of the internet; and financial resources. *Supplier relationships* are becoming increasingly strategic (Cousins and Spekman, 2003) and they play an important role in integrating processes via the internet (Porter, 2001). The capacity to craft and maintain trusting and economically viable supplier relationships and to leverage these relationships with the internet requires tacit, complex coordination and communication skills that competitors may find difficult to imitate (Hall, 1993; Winter, 1987).

According to Schroder and Madeja (2004) *customer relationships* are a critical success factor in deploying the internet. Keller-Johnson (2002) argues that companies that already excel in managing customer relationships seem best equipped to take advantage of the internet's opportunities. Zhu, Kraemer and Xu (2002) found that a lack of trading partner readiness to deploy the internet is a significant internet adoption inhibitor. Within RBV logic, *supplier driven e-business* can be seen as a valuable strategic asset for small firms. Consumer readiness is an internet adoption driver (Zhu and Kraemer, 2002) and, like supplier-driven e-business, *customer-driven e-business* can be seen as a strategic asset for small firms.

Benchmarking is a widespread practice for the development of IT systems (Whitley, 1992). Teo and Choo (2001) reported that using the internet had a positive impact on the quality of competitive intelligence and firm performance. *Strategic use of the internet* can lead to competitive advantage because production and procurement can be more effective and buyers will value a combination of on- and off-line services. Small companies usually have fewer *financial resources* than larger ones, and this lack often limits their opportunities (Caldeira and Ward, 2003; Chow *et al.*, 1997). In contrast, small companies that have access to financial resources, for example via inter-organisational links, can create competitive advantage (Delmas, 2002). The availability of financial resources is also related to IT success (Igbaria *et al.*, 1998; Palvia and Palvia, 1999). It is therefore suggested that:

Hypothesis 1b: Business resources explain significant financial performance variance among small firms.

Dynamic capabilities

For Eisenhardt and Martin (2000) dynamic capabilities comprise specific organisational processes such as product development, alliancing and strategic decision making. These processes are applied to firm-specific strategic assets to create value. This will differ according to the degree of market dynamism. For example, in moderately dynamic markets where change occurs within a stable industry structure, dynamic capabilities resemble routines (Nelson and Winter, 1982). Here dynamic capabilities are complicated analytical processes and rely extensively on existing knowledge and linear execution to produce predictable outcomes. In contrast, in high-velocity markets, dynamic capabilities are simple, experimental and unstable processes that rely on rapidly created new knowledge and iterative execution to produce adaptive, but unpredictable, outcomes.

Today's fast changing markets force firms to respond quickly and to be innovative. Specifically, the following three dynamic capabilities are necessary. First, firms need the capability to learn quickly and to build strategic assets.[2] Second, new strategic assets, such as knowledge, technology and customer feedback, have to be integrated within the company. Third, existing strategic assets have to be transformed or reconfigured (Teece *et al.*, 1997; Eisenhardt and Martin, 2000). These capabilities are discussed fully in the next chapter (Chapter 5) when we examine the development of dynamic capabilities. At this stage, we postulate the following:

> Hypothesis 1c: Dynamic capabilities explain significant financial performance variance among small firms.

Table 4.1 operationalizes these independent variables for the purposes of this research

Complementarity of IT assets

Another core assumption of the RBV is that resources can be complementary. Teece (1986: 301) suggests that complementary assets are especially important for small companies because, in contrast to their larger competitors, they 'are less likely to have the relevant specialized and co-specialized assets within their boundaries and so will either have to incur the expense of trying to build them, or of trying to develop coalitions with competitors/owners of the specialized assets'. Delmas (2002) showed that inter-organisational links to gain access to complementary assets (such as financial resources) can be a source of competitive advantage for small companies.

Empirical research on the complementarity of strategic assets can be divided into two research streams. One stream of research focuses on

Table 4.1 The independent variables

Business resources	
Relationships	Open and trusting relationships with customers and key suppliers
External-driven e-business	Encouragement and support by suppliers and customers to adopt the internet that may create inter-organisational efficiencies
Benchmarking	Actively researching and observing best practices of other firms in activities or processes that need improvement.
Strategic use of the internet	The internet strategy supports and enhances the overall competitive strategy
Financial resources	The necessary financial resources are available
Dynamic capabilities	
Integration	Capability to coordinate internal and external activities
Learning/building assets	Capability to improve task fulfilment and build strategic assets
Reconfiguration	Capability for internal and external transformation and reconfiguration
IT assets	
IT knowledge	The extent to which a firm possesses a body of technical knowledge about objects such as computer-based systems
IT operations	The extent to which a firm utilises IT to manage market and customer information
IT objects	Computer-based hardware, software and support personnel

complementarity between separate companies during strategic alliances or mergers and acquisitions. Rothaermel (2001) found that firms focusing on creating competitive advantage through complementarity at strategic alliances outperformed those firms that limited their focus to the exploration of new technologies. In the same vein, Stuart (2000) found that the reputation of a larger firm is a complementary strategic asset for a smaller firm. In particular, an alliance with a larger firm can help a smaller firm to build confidence and attract customers, which can improve the financial performance of both partners.

Lee *et al.* (2001) found that internal capabilities are complementary to linkages with venture capital companies at small technology-based ventures. When Chung *et al.* (2000) examined mergers and acquisitions they found that banks tend to ally themselves with other banks that can complement their weaknesses. Krishnan *et al.* (1997) suggested that complementarity within top management teams (defined as differences in functional backgrounds between acquiring and acquired firm managers) determines post-acquisition firm performance. Similarly, Capron and Pistre (2002) proposed that acquirers earn abnormal returns only when their strategic assets are complementary with the target (or acquired) firm and not if they receive strategic assets from the target firm only .

The second stream of research focuses on complementarity within a company. Powell and Dent-Micallef (1997) examined the complementarity of IT assets with business resources and human resources and came to inconclusive results. Similarly, Song *et al.* (2005) found complementarity between marketing related capabilities and technology related capabilities only in high-technology turbulent environments, but not in low-technology turbulent environments.[3] In the same vein, Zhu and Kraemer (2002) came to inconclusive results when they examined the complementarity of e-commerce capabilities and IT infrastructure for different performance measures at traditional and technology companies. They found complementarity at technology companies in terms of inventory turnover and cost measures but no complementarity in terms of profitability measures.

Furthermore, there were negative relationships to cost measures at traditional companies, indicating that the interaction of e-commerce capabilities and IT infrastructure *increased* the costs. Zhu (2004) repeated the study with some minor modifications in the retail industry and found complementarity between IT infrastructure and e-commerce capability when performance was measured in terms of revenue generation, cost measures and inventory turnover; however he came to inconclusive results in terms of return on assets (ROA).

Whereas research that examines the complementarity of external strategic assets (those that are controlled by other firms) frequently produces convincing results (for example, Rothaermel, 2001; Capron and Pistre, 2002) the inconclusiveness of research which examines the complementarity of internal strategic assets (for example, Powell and Dent-Micallef, 1997; Song *et al.*, 2005) is alarming. A possible explanation for researchers' problems in evaluating the complementarity of internal strategic assets is that this would require a clear distinction between the different strategic assets (the independent variables). In other words, it would be necessary to 'unbundle' the strategic assets that are related to performance. However, considering the unique character of each resource bundle along with its path dependency, causal ambiguity and social complexity, this unbundling process appears to be extremely difficult (Penrose, 1959; Barney, 1991; Rouse and Daellenbach, 1999). We therefore suggest that researchers should pick research settings in which an evaluation of separated strategic assets is more feasible. This has already yielded valuable insights, for example regarding strategic alliances (Rothaermel, 2001; Stuart, 2000) and mergers and acquisitions (Krishnan *et al.*, 1997; Capron and Pistre, 2002).

Black and Boal (1994) suggest three possible types of relationships between strategic assets: First, strategic assets are *compensatory* when a change in the level of one strategic asset is offset by a change in the level of another strategic asset. Second, strategic assets are *suppressing* when the presence of one strategic asset diminishes the impact of another one on performance. Third, strategic assets are *complementary* when one strategic asset magnifies the impact of another strategic asset on performance.

Technology (Teece, 1986, Rosenberg, 2000) and IT (Clemons and Row, 1991; Mata *et al.*, 1995; Zhang and Lado, 2001) can be viewed as complementary assets. Clemons and Row (1991) suggest that IT can confer sustainable competitive advantage only if it is used to leverage other strategic assets that are controlled by the firm. They argue that even if IT itself is easy to copy, that may not be the case for firm-specific strategic assets. Therefore controlling complementary strategic assets can be a source of competitive advantage. Thus, although IT *per se* may not provide competitive advantage, firms can use it to leverage or exploit firm-specific strategic assets such as organisational leadership, culture and business processes (Clemons and Row, 1991; Henderson and Venkatraman, 1993). Just as IT software is useless without IT hardware (and vice versa) IT assets may create competitive advantage only in combination with other strategic assets (Keen, 1993; Walton, 1989).

A complementary interaction typically enhances the value of both (or all) strategic assets (Barney, 1991). For example, IT may enable a firm to enhance its supplier relationships, while the pre-existing supplier relationships maximise the IT's inherent information-sharing capabilities. The IT would be a commodity resource, yet it may combine with supplier trust to produce an embedded, mutually reinforcing, advantage producing bundle of strategic assets (Powell and Dent-Micallef, 1997).

Powell and Dent-Micallef (1997) examined the complementarity of IT assets with other strategic assets by ranking all firms on their IT assets scores and dividing them at the midpoint into two sub-samples, labelled IT-leading and IT-lagging firms. They suggest comparing IT-leading and IT-lagging companies in a three-step approach for analysing complementarity. First, the average scores of the other strategic assets (business resources and human resources) of IT-leading companies should be higher as a result of the complementarity. Second, the correlation between strategic assets and financial performance should be stronger for IT-leading companies, because IT is used to leverage them. Third, the firm performance of IT-leading companies should be better, because the complementarity enhances the value of strategic assets, and subsequently increases financial performance.

They compared the value of the strategic assets between the IT-leading and IT-lagging companies. It was expected that the IT leading companies would have higher means;[4] however, the actual results were inconsistent (with IT-leading firms having higher means for business resources, but no significant difference in the means of human resources). It was also expected that the correlation between strategic assets and financial performance would be stronger for IT-leading companies than for IT-lagging companies. As expected, human resources had a non-significant relationship to financial performance at IT-lagging firms (r=0.24) and a highly significant effect at IT-leading firms (r=0.57***), and also the business resources of IT-lagging firms (r=0.10) were not significant in contrast to IT-leading firms (r=0.50***). Third, it was expected that financial performance would be better for IT-leading companies, compared to IT-lagging companies. However, against their expectation, IT-leading companies' financial performance was *worse* than that of IT-lagging firms, though the difference was not statistically significant. They concluded, 'With the human and business resources yielding their highest returns in IT-leading firms, these results suggest that ITs do have the capacity to leverage pre-existing intangible resources. On the other hand, the lack of significant performance differences between IT-leading and IT-lagging firms suggests that many IT-leading retailers have not merged these resources successfully.' (Powell and Dent-Micallef, 1997: 392). Whereas there is mixed evidence on the complementarity of IT assets, we still argue that, according to the resource-based logic, complementarity with other strategic assets is plausible. Following Powell and Dent-Micallef (1997) it is therefore hypothesised that:

Hypothesis 2: IT assets are complementary to dynamic capabilities and business resources (see Figure 4.2).

Complementarity of the internet

An uncritical application of the findings of IS research to internet research may be dangerous because of the differences between previous generations of IT and the internet. Although electronic data interchange (EDI) has some features in common with internet-based applications, it is typically more expensive and therefore predominantly used in large companies (Zhu, 2004). The special advantage of the internet is the ability to link one activity with others and make real-time data widely available, both within and outside (Straub and Watson, 2001). Porter (2001: 70) believes that the internet is 'the most powerful tool available today for enhancing operational effectiveness' and thus for lowering costs. By easing and accelerating the exchange of real-time information, it enables improvements throughout the entire value chain. Because the internet is an open platform with common standards, companies can access its benefits with much less investment than was required with previous generations of IT (Porter, 2001) and so SMEs with few financial resources may benefit disproportionately.

In addition, 'within the e-commerce context, the primary system users are customers and suppliers rather than internal users. Customers and suppliers use the system to make buying or selling decisions and execute business transactions' (DeLone and McLean, 2003: 25). internet

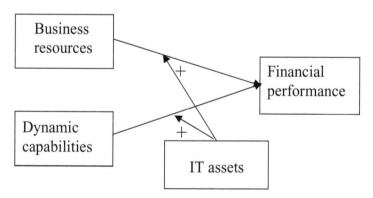

Figure 4.2 Hypothesis 2: IT as a complementary asset

technologies provide better opportunities for companies to establish distinctive strategic positioning (Porter, 2001), the internet can be used to gain access to marketplaces which might otherwise be inaccessible (Rayport and Sviokla, 1995) or it can create new niches (Schmid, 2001). This may enable SMEs to sell their products or services internationally or to find new niche markets (Webb and Sayer, 1998). We therefore suggest that the strategic assets necessary to use IT successfully may not be sufficient to use the internet successfully, and that complementarity between strategic assets and IT assets may differ from complementarity between strategic assets and the internet.

There are two relevant research streams in internet research. One stream of resource-based work aims at identifying and describing strategic assets that are important for virtual markets or e-business. For example, Rindova and Kotha (2001) examined how the organisational form, function and competitive advantage of Yahoo! and Excite dynamically co-evolved. The authors introduced the concept of 'continuous morphing' to describe the comprehensive ongoing transformations through which the firms sought to regenerate their transient competitive advantage on the internet. Dynamic capabilities and strategic flexibility are two organisational mechanisms that facilitate continuous morphing.

Daniel and Wilson (2003) examined the role of dynamic capabilities in e-business transformation of large 'bricks-and-clicks' companies. They identify eight distinct dynamic capabilities associated with e-business transformation. One group is associated with the need for innovation due to the characteristics of the e-business environment, and the second group relates to the need to incorporate or integrate the internet in the existing operations of the business. Tigre and Dedrick (2004) found that industries with strong IT capabilities and a historical orientation towards automation tended to adopt e-commerce earlier.

Another stream of research aims at analysing linkages of strategic assets with firm performance. For example, Zhu and Kraemer (2002) examined the relationship of dynamic capabilities and firm performance and came to inconsistent results for 'traditional' versus 'technology' companies. Zhu (2004) found complementarity between e-commerce capability and IT-infrastructure and a positive relationship to financial performance. Barua *et al.* (2004) found that strategic assets (processes, IT, and customer and supplier readiness) enhance online informational capabilities which then lead to higher operational and financial performance. Barua *et al.* (2004) used the RBV to demonstrate that customer-side digitisation, which is driven by online capabilities and customer readiness, can improve financial performance.

Mata *et al.* (1995) discussed the assertions of asset heterogeneity and asset immobility in the context of IT. They conclude that those IT systems that are used by several competing firms cannot be sources of competitive advantage because the assertion of asset heterogeneity is not met. Further, IT can be a source of sustainable competitive advantage only if firms without IT assets are at competitive disadvantage in acquiring, developing and using IT assets (asset immobility). We argue that the same logic applies analogously to the internet. Then it becomes obvious that the internet does not fulfil either of the two criteria. The internet can be used by any company, and therefore does not fulfil the condition of asset heterogeneity, and the internet is ubiquitous and therefore does not fulfil the condition of asset immobility. Thus the internet itself has no rent-creating potential. This means that the internet itself cannot be a source of competitive advantage. However, it may be possible to use the internet to leverage a firm's existing strategic assets (for example, customer relationships) or to develop valuable skills in deploying the internet. This suggests the following hypothesis:

Hypothesis 3a: The internet is complementary to dynamic capabilities and business resources.

Because the internet itself does not fulfil the assertions of asset heterogeneity and asset immobility it can only be used to leverage strategic assets that do fulfil these criteria. Since neither IT assets nor the internet fulfil the requirements of resource heterogeneity and resource immobility combining these cannot be a source of competitive advantage. Therefore the following null hypothesis is suggested:

Hypothesis 3b: The internet is *not* complementary with IT assets. (See Figure 4.3.)

Research method

Our study examined the direct impact of IT, and the contingent impacts of IT assets and the internet, on the financial performance of firms in different industries, and therefore is consistent with the resource-based view which assumes that performance differences are mainly caused by

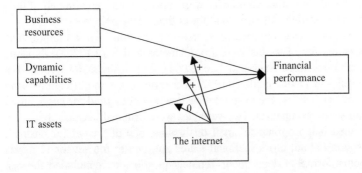

Figure 4.3 Hypothesis 3: complementarity of the internet

firm and not by industry effects (Barney, 1991; Hawawini *et al.*, 2003; Chan *et al.*, 2006). Although Yeoh and Roth (1999) argue that strategic assets are unique for each industry, we believe that, for example, the quality of customer relationships which has been studied in retailers (Powell and Dent-Micallef 1997) or the capabilities of coordination which have been studied in manufacturing companies (Caloghirou *et al.*, 2004) can be valuable for all profit organisations. Furthermore, because the internet blurs and shifts existing market boundaries (Amit and Zott, 2001) differentiation within and between different industries is becoming more difficult even as it is becoming less relevant.

From an original database of 7,600 companies, we identified 2,377 that provided their internet address.[5] After excluding the not-for-profit organisations, 1,963 addresses remained. Fifty companies were used for the pilot. A questionnaire was sent to the remaining 1,913 subjects. Forty-four questionnaires were returned because the companies had gone away or closed, and 11 answered that they would not complete the questionnaire because it was not appropriate for their organisation. This led to a sample of 1,858 companies. Two hundred and twenty-eight questionnaires were returned, and therefore the response rate was 12.3 per cent. After eliminating any remaining not-for-profit organisations, non-independent and too large companies, 146 companies remained. A response rate of 12.3 per cent, although disappointing, is comparable with the range reported in similar studies (for example Provan and Skinner, 1989) and satisfactory considering the requirement of CEO's direct involvement (Lee *et al.*, 2001).[6] On average, 14.4 per cent of company revenues were generated on-line, 22.7 per cent of products and services were procured on the internet, and an average of 22.9 staff were employed. Only four companies were pure dotcoms, creating all of their revenues on-line. All firms had fewer than 250 employees.

All our research measures were taken from the literature. The measures for IT assets were from Tippins and Sohi (2003), dynamic capabilities from Sher and Lee (2004), and business resources from Powell and Dent-Micallef (1997). However, some modifications were necessary because the original measures were designed for large, rather than small, companies. Two variables were dropped because they were deemed inappropriate to small businesses: one of the set for business resources about cross sectional teams and one of the set for IT assets about a formal IT department. Ten new questions were included, the vast majority of them in the dynamic capabilities section according to the suggestions of Caloghirou *et al.* (2004). The final questionnaire can be found in Appendix 1: A.4.1.

Compared with IT assets, usage of the internet was more difficult to measure. We used the construct internet performance (a modification of Powell and Dent-Micallef's IT-performance) and defined as the degree to which firm performance has been improved by the internet. Similar to Zhuang and Lederer (2006), the Powell and Dent-Micallef measures were modified by replacing the impact of IT by the impact of the internet. Therefore, managers were asked about the impact of the internet on their productivity, competitive position, sales, profitability and overall performance.

The financial performance measures were also taken from Powell and Dent-Micallef (1997) and consisted of revenues, sales growth and return on assets. Revenues indicate the company's success in its market transactions, sales growth indicates increasing customer acceptance, and return on assets indicates the management's effectiveness in deploying their assets. Managers were asked if their performance over the past three years was outstanding and if they have exceeded their competitors.

It is broadly accepted that subjective performance measures are highly correlated with the objective ones, and can be used if objective data are not available (Dess, 1987; Dess and Robinson, 1984; Powell and Dent-Micallef, 1997). By using subjective measures it is assumed, given the senior executives involved, that respondents had sufficient perspective and information to assess their firm performance relative to their competitors. Some researchers even prefer subjective measures, because their use reduces the problems of different accounting conventions in areas such as inventory valuation, depreciation, and officers' salaries (Powell and Dent-Micallef, 1997). Ideally, we would have preferred to triangulate reported performance with accounting-based data but small firms are usually held privately and do not provide confidential information as a matter of policy. Even where secondary data are available the organisational structure of the small firm (sole proprietorship, partnership, corporation, and so on) can cause artificial differences. For example it is known that the type of owner compensation on offer can significantly influence the financial performance of small, privately-held firms (Dess and Robinson, 1984).

Research results

To test hypothesis 1 (concerning the direct relationship between strategic assets and financial performance) and following Powell and Dent-Micallef (1997) this linear regression model was estimated:

$$Z_Y = \alpha + \beta_B Z_B + \beta_D Z_D + \beta_I Z_I + \varepsilon$$

Z_Y stands for financial performance, α for the intercept, B for the variable set of business resources, D for dynamic capabilities, and I for IT assets. β_X are the standardised partial regression coefficients for estimating performance Z_Y. According to the hypotheses it is assumed that β_B and β_D will be positive and significant and β_I about zero (Powell and Dent-Micallef, 1997). ε is the residual term that captures the net effect of all unspecified factors.

Table 4.2 shows the Cronbach alphas as a measure for scale reliability. The dependent variables were relatively high with 0.90 for financial performance and 0.95 for internet performance. Cronbach alphas of all variables exceeded the recommended minimum of 0.6 (Bagozzi and Yi 1988), with a range from 0.66 to 0.88 for business resources (overall 0.74), 0.64 to 0.84 for dynamic capabilities (overall 0.87), and 0.61 to 0.92 for IT assets (overall 0.90). All variable sets correlate as statistically significant with financial performance. Correlations for all variables are given as Appendix 1: A.4.2.

Table 4.3 presents the results from multiple regression for the independent variable sets (business resources, dynamic capabilities, and IT assets), the control variable (firm size, 'ln emp' measured as the natural logarithm of employees), and financial performance. The variables combined explain 22.4 per cent of financial performance variance, and an estimated 20.2 per cent of variance in population (using adjusted R^2, which estimates population effects based on sample degrees of freedom).

The significant intercorrelations of some of the sub-variables in the model led us to resolve multi-collinearity problems by dropping variables (Gujarati, 1995). Therefore, additional tests were conducted

Table 4.2 Descriptive statistics

N=146	Alpha	Mean	S.D.	Financial performance
Relationships External driven	0.69	3.97	0.67	0.07
e-business	0.66	2.46	0.99	0.17*
Benchmarking	n.a.	2.72	1.22	0.14
Strategic internet	0.88	3.43	1.14	0.04
Financial resources	n.a.	3.00	1.11	0.51***
Business resources	**0.74**	**3.12**	**0.65**	**0.31***
IT knowledge	0.92	3.33	1.08	0.16*
IT operations	0.87	2.55	0.93	0.25**
IT objects	0.61	3.21	1.01	0.14
IT assets	**0.90**	**3.03**	**0.85**	**0.22***
Integration	0.64	3.69	0.59	0.27***
Learning	0.84	3.63	0.73	0.33***
Reconfiguration	0.68	3.38	0.63	0.38***
Dynamic capabilities	**0.87**	**3.57**	**0.56**	**0.38***
Internet performance	**0.95**	**2.74**	**1.10**	**0.21***
Financial performance	**0.90**	**2.92**	**0.81**	**1**

*** Correlation is significant at the 0.001 level (2-tailed).
** Correlation is significant at the 0.01 level (2-tailed).
* Correlation is significant at the 0.05 level (2-tailed).

Table 4.3 Regression results

	Financial performance
Business resources	0.190*
Dynamic capabilities	0.336***
IT Assets	-0.114
ln emp	0.263***
R	0.473***
R^2	0.224
Adjusted R^2	0.202

*** Correlation is significant at the 0.001 level (2-tailed).
** Correlation is significant at the 0.01 level (2-tailed).
* Correlation is significant at the 0.05 level (2-tailed).

and the results after dropping variables were compared with the results of the construct. We then checked whether dropping variables changed the conclusions of the study. Variables were dropped if they had correlations higher than 0.5 with an included variable (benchmarking, integration, reconfiguration, IT knowledge, and IT objects). The regression analysis with the remaining variables yielded no significant results for the variables relationships, external driven e-business, strategic internet and IT operations. They were therefore also excluded. Thus, in this additional test, business resources were measured only by financial resources, dynamic capabilities by learning, and IT assets were excluded. The results of the regression analysis after dropping variables would not have changed any of the conclusions. We therefore suggest that multi-collinearity is not a problem.[7] Furthermore, the assumptions of multiple regression (normality, linearity, homoscedasticity, and independence of residuals) were examined according to the suggestions of Pallant (2002) and the results suggest that the assumptions were not violated.

The results indicate a direct and positive relationship between business resources and dynamic capabilities with financial performance, but no such relationship between IT assets and financial performance. Thus hypotheses 1a, 1b and 1c were supported.

In order to test the complementarity of IT assets (hypothesis 2) and again following Powell and Dent-Micallef (1997), we conducted a median split for analysing complementarity of IT assets with other strategic assets. We ranked all companies according to their IT assets and divided them into IT-leading and IT-lagging companies. The median was at 3.0, and 73 companies achieved 3.0 or less in their IT asset scores. They were labelled as IT lagging and 73 companies that achieved more than 3.0 were labelled as IT leading.

Powell and Dent-Micallef (1997) used three steps to examine complementarity. First, they compared the means of the independent variables (the strategic assets) between IT-leading and IT-lagging companies. Second, they expected that the correlation between strategic assets and financial performance was stronger for IT-leading companies than for IT-lagging companies. And finally, they expected that financial performance would be better for IT-leading companies than for IT-lagging companies. Our results are shown in Table 4.4. As expected, the means of all independent variable sets (the strategic assets) are higher for the IT-leading companies. Furthermore, the financial performance of IT-leading companies (3.1) is better than that of IT-lagging companies (2.8).

Table 4.4 IT-leading and IT-lagging firms

	IT-lagging (n=73)		IT-leading (n=73)	
	Mean	Standard deviation	Mean	Standard deviation
Business resources	2.8	0.5	3.4	0.6
IT assets	2.3	0.5	3.7	0.4
Dynamic capabilities	3.3	0.5	3.8	0.4
Internet performance	2.3	1.0	3.2	1.0
Financial performance	2.8	0.8	3.1	0.8

Table 4.5 suggests that the relationship between strategic assets and financial performance differs between IT leading and IT lagging companies. Whereas financial performance is strongly related to firm size (measured as the logarithm of employees) at IT lagging companies, dynamic capabilities are strongly related to financial performance at IT leading companies. However, the explanatory power of the model is better for the IT lagging companies (adjusted R^2= 0.200) than for IT lagging companies (adjusted R^2= 0.159). This suggests that the relationship between strategic assets and financial performance is weaker at IT leading companies, which indicates that IT assets are not complementary with strategic assets.

Therefore, hypothesis 2 which suggested complementarity between IT assets and other strategic assets is not fully supported. Although there are some indicators for the complementarity of IT assets (better dynamic capabilities and average financial performance at IT-leading companies) the weaker explanatory power of the model contradicts the existence of

Table 4.5 Regression results

	IT-lagging	IT-leading
ln emp	0.370***	0.130
Business resources	0.129	0.142
Dynamic capabilities	0.263*	0.342**
R	0.483***	0.440***
R^2	0.233	0.194
Adjusted R^2	0.200	0.159

*** Correlation is significant at the 0.001 level (2-tailed).
** Correlation is significant at the 0.01 level (2-tailed).
* Correlation is significant at the 0.05 level (2-tailed).
† Correlation is significant at the 0.1 level (2-tailed).

complementarity. So in order to avoid a Type I error,[8] we must reject hypothesis 2.

To test the complementarity of the internet and strategic assets, we once again followed Powell and Dent-Micallef (1997), ranked the companies according to their internet performance and conducted a median split. The median was at 2.8. Seventy-four companies that achieved 2.8 or less at internet performance were labelled as internet lagging and 72 companies that achieved more than 2.8 were labelled as internet leading.

The results are shown in Table 4.6. As expected, the means of all independent variable sets (the strategic assets) are higher for the internet-leading companies. Further, the financial performance of internet-leading companies is better than the financial performance of internet-lagging companies.

Table 4.6 Internet-leading and internet-lagging firms

	Internet-lagging (n=74)		Internet-leading (n=72)	
	Mean	*Standard deviation*	*Mean*	*Standard deviation*
Business resources	2.8	0.5	3.4	0.6
IT assets	2.6	0.8	3.4	0.7
Dynamic capabilities	3.3	0.6	3.8	0.4
Internet performance	1.9	0.6	3.7	0.7
Financial performance	2.8	0.8	3.1	0.7

Table 4.7 suggests that the relationship between strategic assets and financial performance differs between internet-leading and internet-lagging companies. Whereas performance is strongly related to firm size (measured as the logarithm of employees) at internet-lagging companies, strategic assets are strongly related to financial performance at internet leading companies. Further, the explanatory power of the model is much higher for the internet-leading companies (adjusted R^2= 0.276) than for internet-lagging companies (adjusted R^2= 0.175).

Hypotheses 3a, which suggested complementarity between the internet and business resources and between the internet and dynamic capabilities, was supported. Hypothesis 3b which suggested no complementarity between IT assets and the internet was also supported. We would have expected the relationship between IT assets and financial performance to be non-significant and about zero, as it is for the complete sample (including internet-lagging and internet-leading

Table 4.7 Regression results

	Internet-lagging	Internet-leading
ln emp	0.421***	0.121
Business resources	0.012	0.304*
Dynamic capabilities	0.206†	0.460**
IT assets	-0.071	-0.283*
R	0.469***	0.562***
R^2	0.220	0.316
Adjusted R^2	0.175	0.276

*** Correlation is significant at the 0.001 level (2-tailed).
** Correlation is significant at the 0.01 level (2-tailed).
* Correlation is significant at the 0.05 level (2-tailed).
† Correlation is significant at the 0.1 level (2-tailed).

companies). Surprisingly, the relationship between IT assets and financial performance is *significantly negative* (-.283*) for internet-leading companies. Possible reasons could be that internet-leading companies over-invested in IT assets or that the investments have not paid off yet. This is further discussed in the next section.

Conclusion

This chapter has examined the impact of IT assets and the internet on financial performance. Like most researchers, we were not able to find a direct linkage between IT assets and financial performance (Byrd and Marshall, 2007; Ruiz-Mercader *et al.*, 2006; Zhuang and Lederer, 2006, Neirotti and Paolucci, 2007). This supports our argument that many IT assets are generic and the sole ownership of generic assets cannot be a source of Ricardian rents.

Also like most researchers, we came to inconclusive results when we evaluated the complementarity of IT assets with other strategic assets (Powell and Dent-Micallef, 1997; Song *et al.*, 2005; Zhu and Kraemer, 2002).

Indeed, we have been examining the complementarity of IT assets over several years in a variety of studies. For example, we applied the statistical procedures used in this study to a smaller sample of 106 e-SMEs (used to asses the impact of strategic assets on financial performance and on internet performance; see Schlemmer and Webb, 2006) and came to inconclusive results in terms of complementarity of IT assets, whereas the other results remained the same. We also used different statistical procedures (e.g. hierarchical regression with moderating variables) with both samples, and again the inconclusiveness of the complementarity of IT assets was troublesome, whereas the other results remained relatively stable.

We believe that the reason for the difficulties in examining complementarity of IT assets is that they are deeply embedded in the firm's processes. However, our statistical model actually implies that the strategic assets are clearly separated. Another way to discuss the performance impact of IT assets is shown in Figure 4.4. It is suggested that IT assets are deeply embedded in the organisation, and that they interact directly with other business resources and dynamic capabilities, and that there are no clear-cut boundaries between strategic assets and IT. In this scenario the separation between IT assets and other strategic assets is barely feasible. Yet it is exactly the tight linkages between firm-specific strategic assets and IT assets that can be a source of competitive advantage. Here the unique deployment of IT assets in combination with strategic assets might create a resource bundle that meets the conditions of asset heterogeneity and asset immobility.

This also applies to the complementarity of the internet. The internet is a generic resource that can be accessed by any firm at very low cost and therefore the internet *of itself* cannot be a source of Ricardian rents because the conditions of asset heterogeneity and asset immobility are clearly not met. Yet when we asked the managers how successful they were in deploying the internet we found that internet performance differed greatly between firms. We found that internet-leading companies perform better financially and typically control stronger business resources and dynamic capabilities than internet-lagging firms.

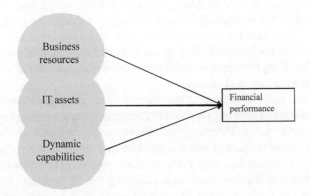

Figure 4.4 Embedded IT assets

In other words, we found some complementarity between strategic assets and the internet in our data. This suggests again that a generic asset can be used to leverage firm-specific assets such as business resources and dynamic capabilities and that this results in superior firm performance.

However, we did not find any complementarity between the internet and IT assets. Indeed, in our study the relationship between the internet and IT assets was significantly negative at internet-leading companies. As already suggested in the literature review, research on the relationship between IT assets and financial performance is frequently inconclusive, but negative relationships are quite untypical (Wade and Hulland, 2004), and according to the resource-based logic, we would have expected no direct relationship between IT assets and financial performance (Mata *et al.*, 1995). However, our results are similar to the original study which suggested that financial performance of IT-leading companies was lower than financial performance of IT-lagging companies (Powell and Dent-Micallef, 1997). We propose two possible explanations for this finding.

First, the internet-leading companies may have over-invested in IT assets. Song *et al.* (2005) suggested 'clearly, resource combinations do not always lead to synergistic performance impact and managers should avoid over investing in contexts where resources cannot be leveraged through configuration, complementarity and/or integration. In terms of resource-based theory, synergistic rents cannot always be obtained' (2005: 271). We have suggested that following the resource-based logic, IT assets and the internet cannot be complementary because neither of them fulfil the criteria of resource heterogeneity and resource immobility. Further, we have demonstrated this in our empirical research. However, this relatively sophisticated resource-based logic may be difficult to understand for managers of small firms, who perform many activities with less expertise than larger companies, because the small firms do not have functional specialists (Verhees and Meulenberg, 2004). Therefore, there appears to be a temptation for managers of small firms to over-invest in IT assets.

A second possible reason for the negative relationship could be that the IT investments have not yet paid off. Performance was evaluated over the past three years. However, the internet and e-business are still relatively young areas, and many companies may be in an early stage, and it may take more time until the investments pay off. This explanation is consistent with the view outlined in Chapter 2 that IT is essentially an endogenous technology that takes many years before its benefits can be measured. It is also consistent with a cautious interpretation of the IT productivity paradox and with the notion that IT is an embedded, firm-specific strategic asset that can interact with other strategic assets to create competitive advantage – but that this process takes time.

For managers, our conclusions caution against an over-investment in generic IT assets. Assets that can easily be purchased by any competitor cannot be a source of competitive advantage. Therefore, competitive advantage by IT is not 'for sale'. However, if IT or the internet is deeply embedded within the firm such that the technology is complementary with other strategic assets they can be a source of competitive advantage. This raises the importance of IT management. Where competitive advantage cannot be obtained from the mere selection and ownership of resources, then the development, use and management of those resources become crucial. In the next chapter we will discuss the potential of IT assets to create Schumpeterian rents through an examination of the process of developing dynamic capabilities and in Chapter 6 we draw out the implications of our analysis for IT management in general.

5 IT and the creation of Schumpeterian rents

Introduction

Teece and his co-authors (1997: 509) position their research 'in a Schumpeterian world of innovation-based competition, price/performance rivalry, increasing returns, and the "creative destruction" of existing competencies'. In Chapter 4 we showed that even in a moderately dynamic environment IT assets may not be a source of Ricardian rents because they do not meet the conditions of resource heterogeneity and immobility. However, IT can be deployed as a complementary asset and therefore may become a source of Schumpeterian rents. In this way IT works along with other strategic assets to confer a competitive advantage on the firm. Yet it is difficult to establish exactly how or why this happens. Critical path dependency makes it difficult for researchers to unravel bundles of interdependent strategic assets and to establish causality in a complex set of inter-relationships.

Rouse and Daellenbach (1999) praise Powell and Dent-Micallef's (1997) research because it 'brings us a long way in understanding the limits of specific, technology-based, competitive advantages' but caution that it 'only suggests where "real" advantages lie' and that although 'we are left convinced that competitive advantage must lie within organisational processes – we do not know the what, how, when, why or where of those advantages' (1999: 491). Since our research reported in Chapter 4 (and elsewhere, in Schlemmer and Webb, 2006) is based on the Powell and Dent-Micallef framework we stand similarly accused. The purpose of this chapter then is to investigate empirically some of these process questions. Specifically we seek to explain the development of dynamic capabilities, to examine the role of leadership and innovation in that process, and to apply this understanding to an examination of the relationship between IT and competitive advantage.[1]

Rouse and Daellenbach (1999) make the important, if often overlooked, point that answers to such process questions cannot be found using positivist research methods. They say that 'while strategic management research during the last two decades has shifted from a focus on environmental factors to intangible resource-based factors in the search for sources of sustainable superior performance, the dominant research approach has not changed significantly'. Moreover, 'it is unlikely that any conclusive findings on competitive advantage will emerge from large-sample studies that indiscriminately include low and typically average-performing firms which the competitive advantage literature and RBV of the firm suggest do not have any sustainable advantage'.[2] Other approaches are needed and they suggest the use of 'in depth fieldwork or ethnographic study methods' because 'given our contention that sustainable advantages are organizational in origin, tacit, highly inimitable, socially complex, probably synergistic, embedded in process, and often driven by culture, there can be no other way to obtain data of interest' (1999: 489).

Accordingly, in this chapter we are concerned with smaller scale, qualitative studies of firm performance. We contextualise our study of owner-managers in the literature on organisational culture and behaviour. Rouse and Daellenbach (acknowledging Lado and Wilson, 1994) note that 'the RBV is fundamentally an enactment-based view of strategy formation and implementation in which firms are seen to proactively manage and shape their environments and not simply respond to exogenous uncontrollable forces' (1992: 492). In this chapter we apply enactment theory to the study of the development of dynamic capabilities. We seek to better understand the processes through which dynamic capabilities are developed and the crucial role played by owner-managers. Then we relate our analysis to the broader concepts of leadership and innovation. This chapter provides an insight into Schumpeterian rent creation in small firms and the role of IT in that process. Chapter 6 then builds upon these insights and those into Ricardian rent creation found in Chapter 4, to compare and contrast two economic paradigms of IT management.

Dynamic capability enactment

It has been suggested that top executives are not equally open to organisational change (Harrigan, 1985; Pettigrew, 1985; Geletkanycz, 1997) but 'rather, many develop a strong personal attachment to existing policies and profiles which support it' (Geletkanycz, 1997: 615). Executives' commitment towards the status quo may be caused by their 'belief in the enduring correctness of current organizational strategies and profiles'. Similarly, Adner and Helfat (2003) suggested that managers could differ in their ability to build, integrate and reconfigure strategic assets (what we, following Teece *et al.* (1997) and Eisenhardt and Martin (2000), call dynamic capabilities) without further discussing what these differences are and how they affect the organisation. In the same vein, Rosenbloom (2000: 1102) concludes from a longtitudinal case study of NCR that 'leadership deserves closer examination and may well be a central element in dynamic capability'. In particular, he suggests that CEOs' commitment towards dynamic capabilities created competitive advantage during periods of rapid market change.

Tripsas and Gavetti (2000: 1158) 'believe that understanding how capabilities evolve cannot neglect the role of managerial cognitive representations'. Boone *et al.* (2000) argued that, especially in small companies, firm and managerial factors merge due to the high internal locus of control exerted by the owner-manager. Similarly, Jones (2004) suggested that in small companies organisational learning and change depend heavily on the owner-manager. Forbes (2005: 357) agrees that managers' decision practices are more strongly associated with performance at small than at large firms, and that at SMEs 'the potential for individual characteristics to influence firm behaviour is especially great [because] in large firms the group dynamics of large top management teams can mitigate the influence of individual cognitive factors on organizational decision making'. We therefore argue that the owner-manager plays a critical role in shaping dynamic capabilities at an organisational level in small firms (Rosenbloom, 2000; Adner and Helfat, 2003) and that the attitudes of managers can enhance (or reduce) a firm's dynamic capabilities (Delmas, 2002).

Lado and Wilson (1994) and Rouse and Daellenbach (1999) claim that the RBV is fundamentally an enactment-based view of strategy formation and implementation and we suggest an 'enactment' between managers' commitment towards the development of dynamic capabilities, organisational dynamic capabilities and financial performance. Weick (1979) developed the concept of enactment, which assumes that managers act upon the environment, interpret environmental responses to their actions and reshape their actions based on the environmental feedback. In particular, managers create mental representations of their environment based on inferences about the effects of their actions. Environmental feedback to their actions changes managers' cognitions. In other words, 'this perspective emphasises the reciprocal link between cognition and action; enactment implies that taking actions produces cognitions, which then guide further action. The process of enactment consists in the ongoing adjustment of an organization's actions and cognitions through its interaction with its environment' (Danneels, 2003: 560).[3]

Rindova and Formbrun's (1999) case study on IBM suggested that managers' interpretations of competitive interactions affect their decisions on how firms deploy strategic assets. Osborne *et al.* (2001) showed that the commitment of the CEO towards research and development and marketing determines company performance in those areas. They postulate a 'progression from plans, to actions to performance, to a new round of plans, to new results' (2001: 449). Similarly, Danneels (2003) examined the customer orientation of retail managers and discovered that in the enactment process cognitions and actions reinforce each other and become increasingly focused.

Therefore we propose a framework (see Figure 5.1) which assumes that CEOs differ in their commitment towards the enhancement and development of dynamic capabilities (Geletkanycz, 1997; Rosenbloom, 2000; Adner and Helfat, 2003) and that commitment towards dynamic capabilities determines the actions that managers take to enhance dynamic capabilities (Weick, 1979; Daft and Weick, 1984; Ocasio, 1997; Bogner and Barr, 2000; Chattopadhyay *et al.*, 2001; Danneels, 2003). A strong or weak commitment towards dynamic capabilities enhances or reduces the development of dynamic capabilities and creates competitive advantage or disadvantage.

The enactment perspective further suggests not only that decision makers act on a mental model of their environment but also that actions

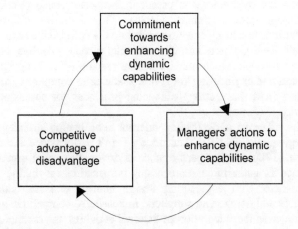

Figure 5.1 Dynamic capabilities enactment

feed back into the mental model on which they are based. This leads to a self-reinforcing feedback loop between commitment, actions and competitive advantage (Weick, 1979; Osborne *et al.*, 2001; Danneels, 2003). Commitment can be defined as 'a state of being in which an individual becomes bound by his actions and through these actions to beliefs that sustain the activities and his own involvement' (Salancik, 1982: 62).

Dynamic capability development

In our research, following Teece *et al.* (1997) and Eisenhardt and Martin (2000), dynamic capabilities were disaggregated into (1) learning and building assets, (2) integrating assets and (3) reconfiguring assets. Learning is the process by which repetition and experimentation enable tasks to be performed better and quicker. It also enables new production opportunities to be identified. In the context of the firm, learning has several key characteristics. It requires common codes of communication and coordinated search procedures. The organisational knowledge generated resides in new patterns of activity, in 'routines', or a new logic of organisation. Routines are patterns of interactions that represent successful solutions to particular problems. These patterns of interaction are resident in group behaviour and certain sub-routines may be resident in individual behaviour.

Collaborations and partnerships can be a source for new organisational learning, helping firms to recognise dysfunctional routines, and preventing strategic blind spots. Learning capabilities are crucial in industries such as pharmaceuticals and optical disks, where cutting-edge technology is essential for performance (Helfat, 1997; Henderson and Cockburn, 1994). This includes alliances and acquisitions that bring new resources into the firm from external sources (Gulati, 1999). Cisco has, for example, a very effective acquisition process through which managers have assembled a changing array of products and engineering know-how that creates competitive advantage. Biotech firms have strong alliancing processes for accessing outside knowledge (Powell *et al.*, 1996).

The effective and efficient internal coordination or integration of strategic assets may also determine a firm's performance. According to Garvin (1988) quality performance is driven by special organisational routines for gathering and processing information, for linking customer experiences with engineering design choices and for coordinating factories and component suppliers. Increasingly, competitive advantage also requires the integration of external activities and technologies, for example in the form of alliances and the virtual corporation. Zahra and

Nielsen (2002) show that internal and external human resources and technological resources are related to technology commercialisation.

Product development routines by which managers combine their varied skills and functional backgrounds to create revenue-producing products and services are an example of integrative capabilities (Helfat and Raubitschek, 2000) which helped Toyota to achieve competitive advantage (Clark and Fujimoto, 1991). Strategic decision making is another integrative capability in which managers pool their various business, functional and personal expertise to make the choices that shape the major strategic moves of their firms (Eisenhardt, 1989).

Fast changing markets require the ability to reconfigure the firm's asset structure and to accomplish the necessary internal and external transformation (Amit and Schoemaker, 1993). Change is costly and so firms must develop processes to minimise low pay-off change. The capability to change depends on the ability to scan the environment, to evaluate markets, and to quickly accomplish reconfiguration and transformation ahead of the competition. This can be supported, for example, by decentralisation, local autonomy and strategic alliances. Transfer processes, including routines for replication and brokering (Hansen, 1999), are an example of reconfiguration capabilities. They are used to copy, transfer and combine strategic assets within the firm. For example, at the premier product design firm, IDEO, managers routinely create new products by knowledge brokering from a variety of previous design projects in many industries and from many clients (Hargadon and Sutton, 1997). Resource allocation routines are used to distribute scarce resources such as capital and manufacturing assets within the firm (Burgelman, 1994). At a more strategic level co-evolving includes the routines by which managers reconnect webs of collaborations among businesses (Eisenhardt and Galunic, 2000). For example, Disney has co-evolved to create shifting synergies that drive superior performance (Wetlaufer, 2000). 'Patching' is a strategic process based on routines to realign the match-up of businesses and their related resources to changing market opportunities (Eisenhardt and Brown, 1999). Dell's constant segmentation of operating businesses to match shifting customer demands is an example of a superior patching process (Magretta, 1998). Furthermore, exit routines that jettison resource combinations that no longer provide competitive advantage are also necessary to achieve sustained competitive advantage (Sull, 1999). Further examples for dynamic capabilities and their enablers are shown in Table 5.1.

Table 5.1 Examples of dynamic capabilities and their enablers

Dynamic capability (Teece et al., 1997)	Of (= examples)	By (= enablers)
Integration is the coordination of internal and external strategic assets.	Teece *et al.* (1997) and Eisenhardt and Martin (2000): • Customer feedback on different stages of the value chain • new technologies in organisational processes • stakeholders (for example alliancing and partnering with suppliers or other companies) • new knowledge in the organisation	Verona and Ravasi (2003): • Fluid project-based organisation • Interaction between experts of different professional areas • Cross-functional teams • Reduction of physical and structural barriers
Learning and building strategic assets. Learning is a process by which repetition and experimentation enable tasks to be performed better or quicker. It also enables new production opportunities to be identified. The organisational knowledge generated by such activity resides in new patterns of activity, in 'routines' or a new logic of organisation.	Eisenhardt and Martin (2000) • Internal and external strategic assets Zollo and Winter (2002): • Operating routines	Teece *et al.* (1997) and Eisenhardt and Martin (2000): • Experimentation • Collaborations and partnerships • Developing individual and organisational skills • Joint contributions of employees
Reconfiguration of the firm's asset structure and the accomplishment of the necessary internal and external transformation.	Teece *et al.* (1997) and Eisenhardt and Martin (2000): • Strategic assets • Organisational structure • Routines	Verona and Ravasi (2003) • Open and informal culture • Openness to individual proposals and creativity • Broad involvement in strategic process Teece *et al.* (1997) and Eisenhardt and Martin (2000): • Reduction of costs for change • Exit routines

Research method

Rouse and Daellenbach (1999: 489) suggest an approach to resource-based research 'that extends, complements, and builds upon common methods that have dominated strategy research, but adds richness of detail, with the potential to reveal the differences, strengths and sources of sustainable competitive advantage'. In particular, they suggest the following methodology:

1 Select an industry
2 Identify a performance hierarchy within the industry
3 Classify firms into high, medium and low performers
4 Focus on the high and low performers
5 Compare the high and low performers using qualitative methods.

This methodology is intended to identify companies that have some common characteristics but that differ significantly in their performance. The first step involves the use of quantitative data to select an industry and to identify companies of similar size. The second step in firm selection is to compare performance indicators within industries. We used our original dataset (Chapter 4) to determine industry type and then used the financial performance data obtained from our postal survey (Chapter 4) to identify high and low performers within each industry.

Financial performance was measured as the managers' perceptions (on a 5-point Likert scale) of revenues, sales growth and return on assets (see the survey questionnaire in Appendix 1: A.4.1). The minimum performance was 6 (= 6 questions * 1 point) and the maximum performance was 30 (= 6 questions * 5 points). The company with the lowest financial performance had 6 points and the best performing company had 29 points; the mean was 17.47 (with a standard deviation of 4.99). The companies were divided into the following three groups: Low performers (6–13 points), medium performers (14–21 points), and high performers (22–29 points).

The greatest differences between the best and the worst performers were found in the IT industry and in the retail industry, therefore companies from these industries were examined. Two high performers and one low performer in each industry agreed to participate in the interviews. Of course, we wished to conduct more interviews, particularly in low performing firms, but many of them had already gone out of business or did not want to participate in this aspect of the research. The key characteristics of the high and low performers are summarised in Table 5.2.

Table 5.2 High and low performers

	Financial performance	Variance	Employees	Turnover
High-IT 1	23	+5.5	8	£ 600,000
High-IT 2	24	+6.5	6	£ 350,000
Low-IT	11	-6.5	10	(unknown)
High-Retailer 1	24	+6.5	7	(unknown)
High-Retailer 2	29	+11.5	8	£ 2,000,000
Low-Retailer	11	-6.5	8	(unknown)

The questionnaire is included as Appendix 2: A.5.1. The questions were sent to the managers beforehand. Each interview took about one hour (ranging from 45 to 90 minutes). The interviews were conducted at the working place of the managers. This enabled the researchers to get a picture of the individual and workplace and to be involved in the actual experiences of the participants (Rossman and Rallis, 1998). A literature search was conducted in tandem with data collection and analysis in order to ground the analysis. In addition interview data were triangulated through a qualitative content analysis of the companies' websites. These data were primarily used to verify interview data and thus increase the validity of the findings (Silverman, 1993).

The interview transcripts were analysed through the categorisation and analysis of emergent concepts and ideas and constant comparison of these concepts to identify common themes (Miles and Huberman, 1984). In contrast to the previous chapter where we compared dynamic capabilities with strategic assets, in this chapter we were concerned to examine how the strategic assets of the original Powell and Dent-Micallef framework (human resources, business resources and IT assets) are built, integrated and reconfigured (which we equate with dynamic capabilities).[4] A framework for this analysis is shown in Table 5.3.

In the original Powell and Dent-Micallef framework, business resources consisted of a variety of sub-categories and variables (e.g. customer relationships, supplier relationships, external driven e-business), but we took the expedient of measuring only one of these, the business resource–customer relationship. This relationship was clearly important to the owner-managers we interviewed and (unlike, for example, financial resources) they were happy to talk about it at length.[5]

As suggested by Miles and Huberman (1984) codes were created from the literature before the fieldwork. Dynamic capabilities were divided in the three sub-categories building (bui), integrating (int) and reconfiguration (rec), and the examined strategic assets were human

Table 5.3 Strategic assets and dynamic capabilities framework

DC \ Strategic assets	Human resources	Customer relationships	IT assets
Building/learning			
Integration			
Reconfiguration			

resources (hr), customer relationships (cu) and IT assets (it). The codes are shown in Table 5.4. Appendix 2: A.5.2 gives an example of a coded interview for this stage. The transcripts of the high and the low performers in the same industry were analysed using the constant comparative method (Strauss and Corbin, 1990); that is, the transcripts were searched using the same codes and the results directly compared in order to establish commonalities and differences.[6]

Table 5.4 Codes for analysing how companies differ in their dynamic capabilities

Dynamic capability	Strategic assets	Codes
Building	human resources	bui-hr
	customer relationships	bui-cu
	IT assets	bui-it
Integration	human resources	int-hr
	customers relationships	int-cu
	IT assets	int-it
Reconfiguration	human resources	rec-hr
	customer relationships	rec-cu
	IT assets	rec-it

The managers' involvement in the enhancement process of dynamic capabilities was also examined. The codes for this emerged progressively during data collection and measured how managers differed in their commitment towards the enhancement of dynamic capabilities and in their subsequent activity of enhancement. The codes for commitment and activity are shown in Table 5.5.

Research results

Our findings suggest that managers of high- and low-performing firms differ in their commitment towards learning and building, integrating and reconfiguring strategic assets. The managers of the high-performing firms were strongly committed towards learning and building strategic

Table 5.5 Codes for the manager's role in enhancing dynamic capabilities

Dimension	Dynamic capability		Codes
Commitment towards	building integrating reconfiguring	strategic assets	com-bui com-int com-rec
Activity in	building integrating reconfiguring	strategic assets	act-bui act-int act-rec

assets. For example, they were committed to enhancing human resources, whereas learning had a low priority for the managers of the low-performing firms. The strong commitment towards learning occurred on an individual as well as on an organisational level. For example, the owner-managers participated in training courses to enhance marketing and team-building capabilities. The manager of a high-performing retailer, who came from a training background herself, said: 'if you stop learning then you become complacent and someone else pips you at the post and we think it's what makes us hungry for the industry'. In contrast, the manager of the low-performing retailer was not committed to learning. He believed that instead of understanding market trends and customer wishes it would be more important to 'educate' customers, so that they buy the products he wants to sell. In addition, the managers of low-performing companies gave experimentation a lower priority than the high performers; as the manager of the low-performing company said, 'over the last few years we looked at several things we might do: providing more service, contract management etcetera ... at the minute we realized that what we need to do is focus more on the core products'.

In contrast, the high-performing IT companies developed prototypes of software solutions for their customers and use their feedback to improve them. In addition, they would try to learn from mistakes and 'change ... how we approach the problem, how we provide them [the customers] with a solution ... And we would generally change our process.' In the same way, the manager of the other high-performing IT company said: 'we are all open to learning, not only open to learning, but also taking what's learned and discussing it and seeing if there are other options and better ways'. They were also more willing to co-operate with other companies if their own expertise was insufficient, for example in building IT assets.

The managers of the high-performing firms were also more committed to integrating strategic assets. They were committed to induct new employees, to reduce barriers between teams and to integrate customer feedback. For example, the high-performing IT companies tried to avoid barriers between employees and departments, 'because team building is critical' (High-IT 2). In contrast, neither of the low IT performers was engaged in team building. Managers of the high IT performers were more active in integrating external strategic assets into their company, for example by combing their own IT with the technology of other companies. All IT managers claimed to be working closely with their customers, but the low IT manager had problems integrating his system into the customers' IT and tried to avoid it. In contrast, the manager of High-IT 1 believed that the integration of their technology into the customers' systems would be a key success factor. He said: 'we are able to take each customer's requirements and individualise them and bring together all the necessary parts'. Also High-IT 2 tried to provide a solution for customers' problems. Therefore they developed products that could be used with a standard browser, in contrast to Low-IT, who just wanted to sell their product. The high-performing companies actively tried to get customers involved in integrating new technology and took an active role in team building in order to integrate human resources. In contrast, managers of the low-performing firms tended to avoid or minimise cooperation.

Managers of high-performing firms closely monitored the market and were willing to change (re-configure) their organisational structure, processes, products and services. They were committed to tailoring their offers according to changing customer wishes and they offered additional services, often in the form of service packages. Further, they matched their IT assets to the changing business structures and processes. In contrast, managers of the low-performing firms frequently tried to avoid changes.

The managers of both high-performing IT companies tried to improve business processes and asked questions such as 'how can we mould things to actually make them operate better?' (High-IT 1). He believed that 'if you cannot accept change and you cannot work with change then there is no point in being in this business and you can go home and close the door immediately'. Similarly, the manager of High-IT 2 was committed to find out 'how we can improve the process' and he asked himself 'is the process that we are following for this project successful? Are we failing anywhere? Is it going more slowly or quickly than expected?' In contrast, the manager of Low-IT showed a high resistance to change. Not only did he avoid changes at the organisational level, he even resisted changes at the product level ('we try to avoid changes to the product'). In contrast High-IT 1 offered a variety of standardised product packages and tailored the products especially to customer needs. The manager said 'nothing is set in stone … we are able to take each customer's requirements and individualise'. Similarly, the manager of High-IT 2 stated that rather than expecting customers to adapt to their products they would modify their products and services to meet customer requirements.

Table 5.6 is a summary of the results. Each of the bullet points is a characteristic in which high and low performers differed. For example, managers of all high performers actively participated in training programmes and offered training programmes for their employees, and the low performers did not. Furthermore the high performers regularly engaged in team-building activities and they took a more active role in integrating new employees in the team than the low performers. The high performers also constantly reconfigured the firm's structure and processes and the low performers did not.

In terms of customer relationships the high performers engaged heavily in experimenting and they made sure that their employees had a solid knowledge of the markets for better understanding customer needs. That helped them to acquire new customers and to enhance existing relationships. They also had an open ear and integrated customer feedback in the company. Furthermore they tailored offers to customer needs and offered a bigger range of additional services than the low

Table 5.6 Results

DC \ Strategic assets	Human resources	Customer relationships	IT assets
Building/learning	• Training programmes for managers • Training programmes for employees	• Experimentation • Employees understand markets	• Co-operations with other companies
Integration	• Team building • New employees	• Integrate customer feedback	• Integrate external IT
Reconfiguration	• Structure • Processes	• Tailor offers to customer needs • Additional services	• Matching of IT and business processes

performer. The main difference in managing IT was that the high performers worked much more closely with their customers and they developed strategic partnerships with IT specialists. They also integrated their own IT systems better with those of their customers, where necessary aligning their IT with their customers' business processes.

Our findings are consistent with the literature. Managers are not equally open to organisational change (Harrigan, 1985; Pettigrew, 1985; Geletkanycz, 1997) and some managers are more strongly committed to old strategies and processes than others (Geletkanycz, 1997). The importance of the owner-manager in small companies has been recognised (Boone *et al.*, 2000; Jones, 2004), as has the role of top managers in the enhancement of dynamic capabilities (Adner and Helfat, 2003; Rosenbloom, 2000). In our research the high-performers' commitment and activity towards learning and experimentation resulted in organisational knowledge and highly skilled employees. They had a better understanding of markets and trends and the employees had better skills. The managers' commitment and actions regarding the integration of technology, organisational knowledge and customer feedback enabled them to fulfil customer needs better than their competitors. Finally, managerial commitment towards change and the reconfiguration of assets adapted and improved organisational structure and processes. Continuous improvement enabled them to enhance the product or service and to offer customers more value.

The financial performance of the high-performing companies reinforced their managers' commitment towards enhancing dynamic capabilities. Positive cash flows gave them financial resources for strategic investments and growth, which in turn lead to the development of new strategic assets. Our results suggest a reinforcing feedback loop as follows – a strong commitment towards the enhancement of dynamic capabilities determined actions which lead (or were perceived to lead) to competitive advantage which then reinforced the managers' commitment to such actions. In contrast, the managers of the low-performing firms had a weak commitment to the development of dynamic capabilities. These managers concentrated on projects which they considered crucial and not on the enhancement of dynamic capabilities. For example, when Low-IT was asked about the development of new capabilities and learning he said, 'we don't want to put too many resources in it'. This resulted in competitive disadvantage which reinforced their negative commitment towards dynamic capabilities. One explanation for why managers sometimes 'throw good resources after bad' follows.

Dynamic capability entrapment

The bounded rationality of managers forces them to rely on simplified representations of the world in order to process information (Simon, 1955). These incomplete representations or mental models shape managerial decision making (Tripsas and Gavetti, 2000). Managers differ in their beliefs about the sources of competitive advantage and these beliefs focus their limited attention on some activities to the exclusion of others. Only tasks which are deemed to be important are closely monitored and controlled (Porac *et al.*, 1989; Ocasio, 1997). For example, executives' actions are influenced by the way they monitor the firm's environment through external scanning, interpretation, alternative generation and selection (Mintzberg *et al.*, 1976) and by their perceptions of threats and opportunities (Chattopadhyay *et al.*, 2001). In our research, managers of high-performing firms believed that dynamic capabilities are critical to firm performance and they monitored and controlled these carefully.

Decision making reflects a manager's selective filtering and interpretation of available stimuli which, in turn, are affected by the idiosyncratic lenses of their beliefs, knowledge, assumptions and preferences. A manager's experiences and values affect the shaping of knowledge, assumptions and preferences on which future decisions are based. This inhibits the ability to conceive of different approaches, managers may not be able to create alternative scenarios (Geletkanycz, 1997) and future options may become limited (Salancik, 1982). These limitations can stop managers from realising threats to the firm (Porac and Thomas, 1990) and often lead to an overdue commitment to the current strategy (Salancik, 1982).

Prahalad and Hamel (1990: 83) called this process 'contraction of the opportunity horizon'. The same behaviour was observed among our low-performing managers. They limited their focus on the traditional way of doing business and had a resistance to change. They invested their time, energy and money only in short-term projects and not in the enhancement of dynamic capabilities. For example, the manager of the low-performing IT company stated that the enhancement of dynamic capabilities was not important at the moment. Rather, he was strongly committed to his traditional way of doing business and tried 'to avoid changes'.

Day and Nedungadi (1994) conclude that managers pay selective attention to information and 'define reality in relatively narrow terms'. Current managerial representations will guide future actions and reinforce current beliefs and practices. The problem is that managers may not see, and therefore will not be able to react to, important changes in context. That is, the narrowing of vision inherent in many managerial representations 'may come at the cost of myopia and dulled sensitivity to challenges outside the prevailing framework' (1994: 41). Hodgkinson (1997) found that firms experiencing a down-turn may actually perpetuate this state of affairs, due to the inability of their managers to revise their mental models fast enough to adapt to the changing environment. In an extensive literature review, Staw (1997) identifies five reasons why managers keep on throwing good resources after bad (see Table 5.7).

Similar examples have been reported within the enactment literature. Johnson and Hoopes (2003) examined the impact of sunk costs on the behaviour of managers and suggested that when the cost of changing a 'strategy increases, firms tend to get locked into initial strategies' (2003: 1066). In addition, firms with limited spare financial resources are more concerned about short-term performance than about long-term strategic issues (Chattopadhyay *et al.*, 2001). Our research indicates that managers with limited financial resources avoid fundamental changes. So the relative costs of strategic changes for low performers are higher because they have fewer financial resources and therefore these would require a higher percentage of their budget. While this implies that poor performance hinders change, the same appears to apply to relative risks. If, for example, a high-performing IT company and a low-performing IT

Table 5.7 Reasons for escalation

Reason for escalation	Examples
Project determinants	Chance that further investments turn the losing situation around
	High eventual pay-off
	Lack of alternatives
Psychological determinants	Optimism and illusion of control
	Self-justification
	Framing effects
	Sunk costs effects
Social determinants	External justification and binding
	Leadership norms
Organisational determinants	Inability of organisation to change
	Political powers in the organisation
	Project matches organisational values
Contextual effects	The political, economical, social and technological environment

Source: From Straw 1997

company both wish to develop a new software project, more resources are at stake for the low performer and the relative risk of experimentation (which is a sub-category of dynamic capabilities) is higher.[7]

It is not only firm performance that determines behaviour – firm size is also a contributory factor. Small companies typically have fewer financial resources and less power to change the competitive environment (Chow *et al.*, 1997; Caldeira and Ward, 2003; Ihlstrom and Nilsson, 2003; Gribbins and King, 2004) and thus they tend to 'fall back on well-known strategies' (Chattopadhyay *et al.*, 2001: 951). Jones (2004) argues that the activities and attitudes of owner-managers affect routines and outcomes, especially in small firms. Gans and Quiggin (2003) suggest that the capabilities of small firms are often limited compared with those of larger companies, which typically have a higher stock of managerial resources. In addition, large companies could also increase managerial resources more easily, because they are more experienced and more willing to include additional managers in the company.

Our comparison of high and low performers suggests that high performers show a high commitment to change, are very active in the enhancement of dynamic capabilities, and create competitive advantage, whereas low performers are not committed to dynamic capabilities, are not active in the enhancement process, and create competitive disadvantage. Both scenarios lead to self-reinforcing loops similar to those proposed by McGregor (1960). He suggested that managers' actions are influenced by their assumptions and attitudes and that environmental feedback may reinforce existing assumptions and attitudes. In particular, he suggested that managers' commitment towards their employees determined their leadership style, and this in turn determines how the employees react. He argued that many corporations managed their employees as if they were work shy, and needed constant direction, monitoring, and control (an approach he labelled Theory X), rather than as if they were responsible individuals who were willing and able to take on responsibility and organise their own work (the alternative he labelled Theory Y).

McGregor believed that managers' attitudes are self-fulfilling, because if workers are treated in accordance with such assumptions their behaviour will reflect these assumptions. Thus, if employees are managed as if they operated on Theory X (or Y) then they will react in a Theory X (or Y) manner. McGregor also suggested that the assumptions of Theory X limit innovation, because 'possibilities are not recognised [and] innovating efforts are not taken ... assumptions like those of Theory X permit us to conceive of certain possible ways of organising and directing human efforts, *but not others*. Assumptions like those of Theory Y open up a range of possibilities for new managerial policies and practices' (McGregor (1960: 54) emphasis in the original).

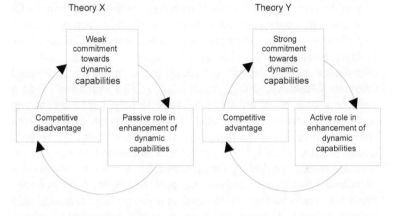

Figure 5.2 Dynamic capabilities enactment and entrapment

McGregor did not link his work to enactment theory. His work is concerned with leadership style and not with dynamic capabilities, and his theory is used here only to present our study's results. As shown in Figure 5.2, managers' strong/weak commitment towards dynamic capabilities may lead to an active/passive role of the manager in the enhancement process, which then leads to competitive advantage/disadvantage, which in turn enhances the strong/weak commitment towards dynamic capabilities.

IT leadership and innovation

It is now time to place this research on the development of dynamic capabilities in the context of the complex relationship between IT and competitive advantage. In particular, the lessons that can be drawn by researchers and managers alike need to be made clear. To summarise from Chapter 3, there are two distinct rent-creation mechanisms within the resource-based view. For those who take the Ricardian perspective, the ownership of resources is the main factor for the creation of economic rents (Barney, 1986b and 1991; Peteraf, 1993; Wernerfelt, 1984). This Ricardian logic has been challenged by the Schumpeterian perspective (Schumpeter and Schumpeter, 1954; Penrose, 1959; Teece *et al.*, 1997), which suggested that innovation and capability-building are the main factors for the creation of economic rents. The Schumpeterian perspective has been codified in the dynamic capabilities framework (Teece *et al.*, 1997; Eisenhardt and Martin, 2000).

The distinction between resources and capabilities cuts directly to the core of the rent creation process. If resources are the primary source for rent creation, managers make their contribution largely through acquiring, possessing and using them. On the other hand, if capability building is the primary source for rent creation, managers make their contribution largely through designing and constructing capabilities internally (Makadok, 2001). Mata *et al.* (1995) examined IT as a possible source of Ricardian rents. They focused especially on two underlying assertions of the RBV: (1) strategic assets differ between competing firms (asset heterogeneity) and (2) these differences are long lasting (asset immobility). They concluded that those IT assets that are used by several competing firms cannot be sources of competitive advantage because the assertion of asset heterogeneity is not met. Further, IT could be a source of sustainable competitive advantage only if firms without IT assets are at competitive disadvantage acquiring, developing and using IT assets (asset immobility).

Whereas the sole ownership of IT assets is unlikely to be a source of competitive advantage, the management of IT assets could be more important. Mata *et al.* (1995) further suggested that, unlike technical IT skills which can be diffused relatively easily among a set of competing firms, managerial IT skills are usually developed over long periods of time through learning and experience. However, since technical IT skills are valuable to the firm, these skills may be a source of temporary competitive advantage, until competitors acquire their own IT skills. Keen (1993: 17) came to similar conclusions: 'the wide difference in competitive and economic benefits that companies gain from information technology rests on a management difference and not a technical difference.' In the same vein, Brynjolfsson and Hitt (2000: 24) believed that 'as computers become cheaper and more powerful, the business value of computers is limited less by computational capability and more by the ability of managers to invent processes, procedures and organizational structures that leverage this capability'. According to Lin (1998), this applies especially to SMEs and he suggested that the managerial skills of SME business founders are more important for organisational performance than technical skills.

We suggest that innovation and capability building are critical factors when using IT to create competitive advantage. Managers can hardly make their contribution through forming expectations about the value of IT resources to their company by acquiring them, and thus receive

Ricardian rents, because the assertions of asset heterogeneity and asset immobility are not met (Mata *et al.*, 1995). Capability building is the primary factor for rent creation with IT assets, and managers make their contribution largely through building, integrating, and reconfiguring IT assets (Makadok, 2001). In contrast to the static equilibrium concept of the traditional resource-based view, the dynamic capabilities framework (Teece *et al.*, 1997) analyses the sources and methods of wealth creation and capture by firms operating in rapidly changing environments. In such conditions, the mere existence of appropriate bundles of specific strategic assets is not sufficient to sustain competitive advantage.

The basic assumption of the dynamic capabilities framework is that today's fast-changing markets force firms to respond quickly and to be innovative. Therefore, the following three dynamic capabilities are necessary. First, in order to meet these challenges, organisations and their employees need the capability to learn quickly and to build strategic assets. Second, new strategic assets, such as knowledge, technology and customer feedback, have to be integrated within the company. Third, existing strategic assets have to be transformed or reconfigured (Teece *et al.*, 1997; Eisenhardt and Martin, 2000).

The dynamic capabilities framework has been applied to IT research (Sher and Lee, 2004) and to internet research. For example, Rindova and Kotha (2001) conducted case studies on Yahoo! and Excite and suggested that the fast-changing virtual markets require dynamic capabilities. Marr *et al.*, (2002) suggest that capabilities are related to performance at e-business companies. Zhu and Kraemer (2002) found an inconclusive relationship between e-commerce capability (a set of measures based on the dynamic capabilities framework) and some measures of financial performance. In his later work, Zhu (2004) found some complementarity between e-commerce capability and IT infrastructure and a positive relationship with financial performance (measured in terms of revenues per employee, inventory turnover and cost reduction). However, he came to inconclusive results in terms of return on assets (ROA).

Sher and Lee (2004) suggested that management of endogenous and exogenous knowledge through IT applications enhances dynamic capabilities. Daniel and Wilson (2003) identified eight distinct dynamic capabilities associated with e-business transformation of 'bricks-and-clicks' companies. They divided these capabilities into two groups. One group relates to the need for innovation due to the characteristics of the internet environment, and the second group is associated with the need to incorporate or integrate the internet into the existing operations of the business. Montealegre (2002) conducted a longitudinal case study of a stock exchange in a developing country. He analysed the development of the internet strategy and discovered three phases: establishing direction, focusing on strategy development, and institutionalising the strategy. Ethiraj *et al.*, (2005) examined dynamic capabilities in a software company at project level. Their quantitative comparison of different projects suggests that client-specific capabilities and project management capabilities drive project profitability.

Verona and Ravasi (2003) examined a leading company in the hearing-aid industry. As in this book, they used Teece *et al.*'s (1997) sub-categories of integration, learning and reconfiguration for dynamic capabilities. Their key argument was that the company created competitive advantage by continuous innovation. Their findings suggested that in order to sustain product innovation a firm must build dynamic capabilities that allow the simultaneous and continuous creation, absorption and integration of knowledge. This requires a long-term commitment to the creation of knowledge, and its transformation into new products and processes. They highlighted the joint use of knowledge creation, absorption and integration as the foundation for continuous innovation.

A context that triggers creativity from all parts of the organisation at any time can support continuous innovation. This context can rest on a loosely coupled arrangement, for example, the distribution of tasks and resources, and the interplay of people at all levels who possess the ability to identify resources and combine them in new ways and to continuously redesign the organisation by redistributing roles, tasks and responsibilities. Dynamic capabilities can be supported by the structure of the organisation. For example, the product development process could eliminate physical and cultural barriers between experts from different departments in order to allocate people, resources and tasks within the organisation as a whole. Verona and Ravasi (2003) examined human and physical resources, structures, systems and company culture as building blocks of product innovation. These assets should coexist and be coherent for the creation of competitive advantage.

Conclusion

From this analysis and discussion we can conclude that the management of IT is important to the achievement of superior firm performance and competitive advantage. But which aspect of management? Clearly the significant role of dynamic capabilities, and the importance of the development of these, makes innovation and leadership essential. This conclusion is based not only upon our own (admittedly limited) empirical study but upon a review of empirical studies into the value of

IT across firms, across industries and across the world. The conclusion is entirely consistent with Schumpeterian theory because it can be seen that the greatest benefits of IT will be realised where there is uncertainty and where leadership and innovation come to the fore. This is not to deny, however, the importance of 'mere' management. Most IT requires management most of the time but mere management alone will not deliver competitive advantage using IT. The full implications of these conclusions are explored in Chapter 6.

6   Conclusions

Introduction

In this book we have examined the relationship between IT and competitive advantage from the perspective of economic theory in general and that of Schumpeterian economic theory in particular. Beginning with a theoretical and *prima facie* case that IT cannot be the source of sustained competitive advantage (because IT is neither heterogeneous nor inimitable), we distinguished between what McAfee (2005) has called the 'raw materials' of IT (hardware, software and networks) and the 'finished goods' of IT (technology that can be used productively to add value). We concluded that although the raw materials of IT are becoming more of a commodity, the finished goods of IT are not. On the contrary, even as IT hardware, software, networks and processes become more of a utility, the use and management of IT resources becomes more, not less, important. Only the use and management of IT can deliver superior firm performance and sustained competitive advantage.

We investigated the direct and indirect impact of IT on firm performance. We concluded that IT had no direct impact on firm performance, but we admit that IT may enable competitive advantage because of its complementarity with other strategic assets.[1] This complementarity derives from, and is given significance by, the role of IT as an endogenous technology. IT is shaped by, and representative of, specific firm resources and capabilities, it is embedded, historically path dependent and causally ambiguous. In this sense IT assets (other than base hardware, software, networks and processes) cannot be considered a commodity. IT continues to be critical to firm performance and to be a legitimate area for strategising, especially in volatile markets.

IT is an endogenous asset which must be managed carefully, and with due consideration of the dual roles performed, during periods of equilibrium (when IT is used to support market positioning and the capture of monopoly rents) and during periods of disequilibrium (when IT is used to innovate and to create sustainable competitive advantage). In turn, these roles require a duality of management approaches, what Schumpeter referred to as 'mere management' on the one hand, and 'leadership and entrepreneurship' on the other.

To a large extent this book has been concerned with exploring how, when, where and why such duality becomes significant in theory and in practice – in a review of the relevant economics and strategic management literatures (Chapters 2 and 3), in empirical investigations (our own, and others) of the relationships between IT and competitive advantage (Chapter 4), and through an investigation of the development of dynamic capabilities (Chapter 5). If managers believe that opportunities for strategy come primarily from resource-based differences and imperfection in an essentially static market structure then they will act in ways that exploit these differences, but will also be constrained by the limitations of this view. If, on the other hand, managers believe that real strategy is formulated during periods of market disequilibrium, or disruption, then they will act to exploit this uncertainty – through innovation, entrepreneurship and leadership. Mathews (2006) has argued that it is only this latter scenario that is of interest to strategy researchers.

Yet it is too simplistic to say that managers will fall readily either into a Classical (Ricardian) or an Evolutionary (Schumpeterian) camp. In practice, managers will exhibit characteristics of both paradigms, at times carefully managing resources in order to exploit resource-based differences or market power in relatively static markets, at other times seeking to exploit market disruption through leadership and innovation during periods of disequilibrium. Nor is each mode of behaviour exclusive to its 'natural' environment. For example, managers may innovate during periods of equilibrium, or near equilibrium, to exploit inefficiencies in market structure and to develop first-mover advantages. During periods of disequilibrium, managers may be concerned to supervise the acquisition and deployment of resources to enable risk taking. Also, good managers will move seamlessly between these modes as circumstances change.[2]

We believe in a duality – not a dichotomy – of management approaches, but nevertheless we believe it is beneficial to identify predominant types. These types may then be used to highlight particular strategies, and combinations of strategies, and their success in generating competitive advantage. Table 6.1 compares and contrasts the two economic and managerial paradigms explicitly and implicitly discussed in this text, and which have informed our interpretation of the impact of IT on firm performance, and of the relationship between IT and competitive advantage.

Table 6.1 Ricardian versus Schumpeterian paridigms

Ricardian paradigm	Schumpeterian paradigm
Rent appropriation by and for the few. Theory of market power, exploiting imperfections in market structure to secure monopoly – but short term – economic rents.	*Rent creation by and for the many.* Theory of innovation and entrepreneurship exploiting uncertainties in the system to create long term, sustainable growth in the economy.
Imperfect equilibrium limits strategy. Strategising is limited to the pursuit of market power during periods of stability and hence is not of much interest to researchers.	*Disequilibrium elevates strategy.* Strategising is concerned with defending and building positions during periods of uncertainty, and hence is of great interest to researchers.
Technology as a means of production limited within equilibrium to short term profit maximisation through exploiting market power.	*Technology as an agent of change* liberated by concept of economic system as evolving to profit seeking through creative disruption.
Risk as a service to factors and not a residual (or profit). It is not possible to earn real profits during periods of equilibrium and this is of limited interest to strategising.	*Uncertainty as part of the residual and therefore profit.* It is only possible to earn real profits during periods of disequilibrium. This is the concern of real strategising.
Profit maximisation in an essentially static environment through the exploitation of market imperfections (and firm resources) to gain market power.	*Profit seeking in an evolutionary environment* through the exploitation of leadership, innovation, entrepreneurship and technology to achieve growth.
Innovation is exogenous and redistributive. Innovation is primarily a reaction to external shocks to the system and the chief purpose of innovation is to manage those shocks to maintain stability.	*Innovation is endogenous and creative.* Innovation is primarily a function of the activities of the firm (its uses of resources and capabilities) and its purpose is to grow the firm by exploiting uncertainties in the marketplace.
Profits result from market power, which results from exploitations of imperfections in market structure to achieve monopoly or economic rents.	*Profits result from innovation*, which is not primarily a position of market power (though it may be used for this purpose to effect short term protection from rivals).
Firm is a profit maximiser based on market power, a price and decision maker, a device for coordination and exchange of established activities.	*Firm is a profit seeker*, a device for experimentation, learning, knowledge creation, and innovation, based on resources and capabilities.
Management is the management of differential resources and market power	*Management is leadership and entrepreneurship generating new wealth through innovation.*

So the Ricardian and Schumpeterian paradigms are presented as two distinct but compatible modes of management behaviour. The relationship between these paradigms is illuminated by considering the role of innovation. According to Schumpeterian theory innovation is a key driver for economic growth. This is not innovation during periods of relative stability when imperfections in the market are exploited to obtain short-term economic rents for the benefit of one or a few firms but innovation during periods of uncertainty, when the opportunities created by that uncertainty are exploited to realise long-term and sustainable growth for the entire economy. Of course exploitation of market imperfections can be important to giving a firm the breathing space necessary in order to exploit long term opportunities, but the distinction between these two realms of activity is clear in economic theory, if not always in management theory (as evidenced by interpretations found in the 'Schumpeterian hypothesis').

Innovation can create new wealth through entrepreneurial action and disruption. Innovation can also maximise profits through market power. In this book we have emphasised the former over the latter but both are features of the modern firm. Innovation of either kind is determined by firm capabilities, resource bundles, complementarities and absorptive capacity, and the difference between innovation and imitation is difficult but none the less important to identify. Whereas innovation has received most attention in the literature, increasing attention is being paid to the role of imitation in creating competitive advantage. To an increasing extent, empirical evidence is showing that innovators as first movers do not always, or even normally, benefit most from an innovation (for example, see Clemons and Row, 1991; Rosenberg, 2000; Smith *et al.*, 2001). This implies that the ability to understand and apply an innovation may be more important than the ability to create and develop it. Clearly in this context, management may be more important than entrepreneurship.

This has important implications for the study of the impact of technology on firm performance. If firm success is determined as much by technological imitation as by technological innovation (or even more so) then it will be more difficult to account for each type of success. In particular, the benefits accruing from technological change arising out of imitation are likely to be much harder to identify and measure because imitation takes place over a much longer timeframe, and is inherently more complex. This is one explanation why the results of research investigating the impact of IT on firm performance have been so disappointing, and why the literature continues to discuss the IT productivity paradox.

Furthermore, because technological imitation is closely linked to absorptive capacity, and because a firm's absorptive capacity is crucially determined by the resources and capabilities at its disposal and how it uses these, IT cannot be a commodity. We argue that in this critical sense IT is no different from the adoption and implementation of any other endogenous technology: it is firm specific, locally embedded, causally ambiguous, rare, heterogeneous, immobile and inimitable. IT is therefore a source of competitive advantage. We have argued that although IT does not directly contribute to superior firm performance, it may do so indirectly as a complementary strategic asset. We have also argued that the effective use of IT as a strategic asset requires both mere management and leadership.

Despite presenting a table (6.1) of differences, we wish to emphasis also the commonalities.[3] We seek a duality of management approaches to the use of IT for competitive advantage, not a dichotomy. The logic of this duality has been established in economic theory (Chapter 2). We have sought to identify this duality, and account for its consequences in the strategic management literature (Chapter 3), and in empirical studies of competitive advantage (Chapter 4). Although we have focused on the role of leadership and innovation in the development of dynamic capabilities (Chapter 5), we have also noted the importance of the management of business, human and IT resources. In further discussion of the nature and importance of this duality we now consider the development of core competences, and the concept of organisational resilience.

Core competences and organisational resilience

Prahalad and Hamel (1990) suggested that companies should seek to develop leadership in selected areas – the so-called core competences.[4] The core competences can be a source of competitive advantage if they fulfil the following three criteria. First, they have to provide potential access to a wide variety of markets. Second, they should make a significant contribution to the perceived customer benefits of the end product. And third, they should be difficult for competitors to imitate. Prahalad and Hamel further argued that companies should focus on only a few (a maximum of five or six) core competences, and then transfer the core competences to core products. They describe Honda as an example of a company that had the core competence to build high-revving, smooth-running, lightweight engines for motorcycles and then exploited this core competence for other markets (for example cars, four-wheel off-road buggies, and boat motors).

A combination of the core competences concept and the dynamic capabilities framework was developed by Hamel and Valikangas (2003) and labelled resilience. Resilience is the ability to dynamically invent and re-invent business models and strategies as circumstances change and is defined as 'the capacity for continuous reconstruction' (2003: 55). Hamel and Valikangas' main argument is that companies should focus on their existing resources but that the continuously changing environment, customer preferences, markets, and competition force them to continuously reconstruct them. It is important to note that they do not recommend replacing these core competences, only extending them. Indeed Hamel and his colleagues (Prahalad and Hamel, 1990 and Hamel and Valikangas, 2003) believed that large companies take unnecessary risks by diversification and that entering markets in which they cannot exploit their core competences would undermine their competitive advantage.

When we applied the resilience concept (Hamel and Valikangas, 2003) to the small IT companies we studied in Chapter 5 we got some interesting results (Webb and Schlemmer, 2006).[5] Resilience was defined as the continuous reconstruction of resources (Hamel and Valikangas, 2003). The reconstruction process was divided into the sub-categories building, integrating and reconfiguring resources. Our interviews with owner-managers indicated that high-performing companies create competitive advantage by resilience, average performing companies create a combination of advantages and disadvantages, and low performers create competitive disadvantages. Our findings suggest that even though the concept of resilience has been developed for large companies, it can also be applied to small ones. Moreover, we believe that the simple structures and the focused strategies of small companies are an adequate research setting for exploring the resilience concept.

However our data also suggest that the Hamel and Valikangas resilience concept, which is based on Hamel's earlier work on core competences and existing resources, may be too narrow. Whereas the concept of core competences has attracted huge interest by practitioners, it has also been heavily criticised by researchers because core competences can also become competency traps (Levitt and March, 1988) or core rigidities (Leonard-Barton, 1992). Leonard-Barton discovered a paradox by showing that while core competences facilitate the development of projects closely aligned with the core business they also inhibit innovation. She called these core rigidities, the dysfunctional flip side of core competences. Thus managers face the dilemma of both utilising and maintaining their core competences, and yet avoiding their dysfunctional flip side by renewing and replacing them.

This paradox is supported by other research. For example, Dougherty (1995) discovered that 'core incompetences' grow around a firm's core competences. This was supported by Henderson's (1993) research which suggested that organisational skills were hampered by incumbents' previous experience. Similarly, Sorenson and Stuart (2000) suggested that greater reliance on prior developments is associated with more innovation (at semiconductor and biotechnology companies) but that this innovation (which relies on internal developments) is less relevant, and is therefore a hallmark of obsolescence. Rosenkopf and Nerkar (2001: 303) found that 'firms that focus inward on their core competences run the risk of developing innovations that wind up being peripheral to the aggregate path of technological development'.

Rosenkopf and Nerkar (2001) also discovered a trade-off between the impact of innovation on the domain of the core business and the overall impact beyond that domain. They argued that innovations based on core competences tend to create domain impacts and subsequently short-term gains, whereas innovations beyond the core competences tend to create overall impacts and subsequently long-term gains. They believed that the reason for the higher impact of innovations outside their core competences could be the usage of external expertise. In particular, by including external expertise, firms can increase the number of choices between different technologies and thus the likelihood of choosing well-regarded technology. In contrast, building on internal expertise restricts that choice.

So the literature supports Leonard-Barton's (1992) suggestion that core competences have to be renewed *and replaced*. But the resilience concept as suggested by Hamel and Valikangas focuses only on renewing and not on replacing. Our own data suggest that a too strong internal focus and ignoring external stakeholders such as customers and partners can be a source of competitive disadvantage. For example, our low-performing firms continuously ignored customer feedback, were not capable of integrating their own IT with customers' systems and subsequently created competitive disadvantages. In contrast, the integration of customer feedback, cooperation with other companies, integrating new employees in the company, and training courses with external trainers, helped the high performers to create competitive advantages (Webb and Schlemmer, 2006).

Our results suggest that the resilience concept (Hamel and Valikangas, 2003) is incomplete, mainly because it does not address

Leonard-Barton's suggestion that core competences have to be replaced since they could otherwise become core rigidities. The main implication for managers is that they should not focus exclusively on core competences. There is a very thin line between a core competence and a core rigidity. Continuous reconstruction of human resources, customer relationships and IT resources is a source of competitive advantage. But managers should also seek to strengthen the resources they control by including external expertise: as Leonard-Barton (1992) suggested, they have to renew *and* replace them, as necessary.

The concept of resilience is based on the earlier concept of core competences which was rooted in the RBV. Prahalad and Hamel (1990) argued that a firm should stick to what it does well. That is, a firm should develop its core competences including extension into new areas (as Honda has done) but should not seek to develop new core competences. Thus the concept of core competences is conservative, and presumes stability or relative equilibrium in the marketplace. As such, core competences are associated more with management than with innovation. However, core competences can become core rigidities when the environment changes. What a firm has been good at in the past may be no longer relevant, and may even become an impediment to competing successfully in the new environment. In such circumstances the firm needs to develop new competences, and to compete in a new way. This requires leadership and innovation rather than management. This new environment is likely to be more volatile and more complex, and requires dynamic strategising.

Yet even here management is still required. First, as the firm develops new competences and begins to make the transition to the new environment, existing core competences, responsible for the previous success of the firm and even now responsible for product cash cows, will have to be managed. Second, the transition itself will require to be managed as existing resources and capabilities are developed to meet the needs of the new market. This implies the judicious acquisition and use of new resources, as well as the management of existing resources. Finally, when the transition is complete, the new combination of strategic assets must be managed until such time as another external shift in the marketplace occurs and the focus switches once more to leadership and innovation.

Schumpeter regarded leadership as a special case of management, and the relationships between leadership and entrepreneurship and between entrepreneurship and innovation are well established and need no further elaboration here. However, it is worth noting that just as management is still relevant in periods of disruption, leadership is still relevant in periods of calm. As we have seen, innovation within the context of equilibrium can give companies a breathing space in which to develop the capabilities and resources, competences and strategies necessary to adjust to the new environment. This is what happens when a firm extends its core competences in new areas but does not (as yet) develop new competences. Here both management and leadership are required to build resilience but also to avoid rigidity. Dualism, not dichotomy, characterises the response.

Exploration versus exploitation of IT

March (1991, 2006) has compared the benefits of exploring new possibilities with the benefits of exploiting old certainties in organisational learning. Exploration includes variation, risk taking, experimentation, play, flexibility, discovery and innovation. In contrast, exploitation includes refinement, choice, production, efficiency, selection, implementation and execution. March believes that firms have to find a balance between exploitation and exploration. If a firm focuses solely on exploration and neglects exploitation, it produces only costs and is not able to gain the benefits. In contrast, if a firm focuses solely on exploitation and neglects exploration, it will be trapped in a suboptimal stable equilibrium.

March (1991) believes that both exploration and exploitation are vital for firm performance but that they compete for scarce resources, forcing organisations to choose between the two. The choice is extremely difficult because the expected values between the options are unknown beforehand, especially in the case of exploration. Compared with returns from exploitation, returns from exploration are more uncertain, more remote in time, and they distract from the firm's core competences. These characteristics 'lead to a tendency to substitute exploitation of known alternatives for the exploration of unknown ones, to increase the reliability of performance rather than its mean. This property of adaptive processes is potentially self-destructive' (1991: 85). Therefore 'the basic problem confronting an organisation is to engage in sufficient exploitation to ensure its current viability and, at the same time, to devote enough energy to exploration to ensure its future viability' (Levinthal and March, 1993: 105).

The concept of exploration and exploitation has been applied to IT research. Garud *et al.* (2006) studied the global IT services company Infosys Technologies which managed to transform itself even as it continued to perform seamlessly on a day-to-day basis, by choosing an organisational design that enables the exploitation and exploration of knowledge simultaneously. In particular, Infosys used day-to-day activities in order to generate new possibilities, thereby ensuring exploration along with exploitation, which was supported by the organisational design, consisting of people, technologies, processes and governance.

Lyytinen and Rose (2006) suggest that in information systems development organisations should conduct exploration activities, such as technology sensing, experimenting, convivial computing, prototyping or user-led innovation; and exploitation activities, such as control, predictability, productivity and repeatability of information systems. Kearns (2007) examined 269 companies that make IT investments in an explorative or an exploitative way. Firms that tended to use IT in an explorative way were more likely to deploy resources for new and unknown technologies and accepted higher risks. In contrast, firms that deployed IT in an exploitative way risked turning core competences into core rigidities. He suggests that those firms that used IT in an exploitative way were less successful in creating a positive IS environment (compared with companies that use IT in an explorative way, or companies that balance their explorative and exploitative IT usage) which reduced IT performance.

These findings are consistent with the research reported in this text. IT assets can be used in an explorative way to create Schumpeterian rents or in an exploitative way to create Ricardian rents. We believe that IT assets are more valuable when creating Schumpeterian rents but it is also possible to create Ricardian rents by leveraging IT assets with other strategic assets. As suggested by March (1991) these different usages have to be balanced carefully, which is consistent with our duality of management approaches.

Further research

If we believe that true competitive advantage is earned during periods of uncertainty, if we accept that this is when and where real strategising takes place, and if we regard IT as a key strategic asset that can be used to improve firm performance, then we are immediately confronted with a series of related questions, none of which have been addressed directly in this text. How best can IT be used to support the sort of dynamic decision making and innovative actions that needs to take place? Can existing theories, models, methods and applications scale up? Or should we be looking for the 'new combinations' that Schumpeter spoke of? If so, what are these? How may they be identified, acquired, built, sustained and reconfigured? Where, when and how does evolutionary strategy meet revolutionary IT?

These are questions that researchers are now beginning to consider. For example, Smith *et al.* (2001) advocate 'competitive dynamic research'. Grounded in Schumpeter's economy theory, competitive dynamics research is the study of how technology supports competitive decision making and actions in a dynamic environment. Of particular concern is the sequence of actions and reactions taken by firms in strategy formulation and implementation, including – but by no means limited to – the roles of leadership, entrepreneurship, innovation and technology.

Interestingly, Smith *et al.* (2001) suggest that even in this new and exciting research stream the old habits of strategic management researchers die hard. Despite being based on Schumpeterian economics and focused on dynamic environments, much of the reported research is locked into equilibrium analysis. Thus in their general overview of the 'basic model and theory underlying competitive dynamics research' (2001: 320) there are frequent references to market distortions, monopoly rents, first-mover advantages and exploiting the time-lag between innovation and imitation. To be fair, their overview is more reflective of the time-lag between the conduct of academic research and its publication.

More importantly, Smith *et al.* (2001) expertly map out an area of future research where the full force of Schumpeterian theory can be brought to bear on the seemingly intractable problems of identifying, explaining and evaluating competitive advantage at firm level. They acknowledge that conducting such research at the level of the small firm is likely to be beneficial because it facilitates the testing and development of RBV and promotes field studies because of the limitations of studying secondary and archived data. We claim a modest contribution in this area. We have studied leadership, entrepreneurship, innovation and technology in the context of small firm strategising, and by extension have 'examined decision making and performance using new theories of action' (Smith *et al.*, 2001: 34) by employing Weick's (1979) theory of enactment (in Chapter 5).

However, it would be remiss of us if we did not remind current and prospective researchers of IT and competitive advantage of the difficulty of the task. Whereas Prahalad and Hamel (1990) hold up Honda as an example of the development and extension of core capabilities, another Japanese automotive manufacturer, Toyota, is held up as an example of a learning organisation, an organisation extraordinarily able to develop new capabilities. The Toyota Production Systems (TPS) is widely revered, frequently copied but never bettered. It appears that even Toyota cannot explain the exact reasons for its success. Toyota's competitive advantage lies in its unique combination of resources and capabilities developed over many years. Yet it is still unclear what that combination is, and how or why it works.[6]

Middleton and Sutton (2005: 93) readily accept that the transition to this type of lean system is not easy ('lean thinking is counter-intuitive and difficult to grasp on first encounter') but argue that it then becomes 'blindingly obvious once the light comes on'. Whether this is true or not – and Middleton and Sutton argue persuasively that lean manufacturing techniques have been applied successfully across a range of industry sectors, including software development – it would seem that many firms still do not get it. What is clear is that many researchers still have difficulty in explaining it. As discussed in Chapters 2 and 3, the inherent difficulty in unbundling bundles of strategic assets may mean that this task remains elusive.

This is not, we should quickly add, an excuse to avoid doing this type of research but, rather, a recognition that this research is never going to be easy. We agree with Middleton and Sutton (2005: 16) when they make clear that the technology alone is never going to provide the answers we all seek: 'techno-centrism, using technology for technology's sake appears to be just another infrastructure that mass producers adopt as a tool to maximise efficiency, once again losing sight of the true purpose of their business'.

Conclusion

In this text we have provided some insights into the theory and practice of management in volatile environments, especially in the small firm context. We have substantiated in empirical data some popular and practical interventions, such as the need to innovate and to manage IT resources carefully. We have promoted a dualism in IT management, emphasising that the strategic use of IT requires both 'mere' management and entrepreneurship. And we have argued that IT is a legitimate and important subject for strategising.

For researchers we offer the following insights. First, the definition of competitive advantage is extremely important because it determines what is measured, how it is measured and the outcomes of the study. We raised this important issue in the opening chapter, and elsewhere (Schlemmer and Webb, 2006) we have examined both aggregate and disaggregate of firm performance. In the research reported in that paper we studied internet performance as a disaggregate measure of firm performance (which was measured as financial performance) and we uncovered important relationships between the internet and strategic assets (business resources and dynamic capabilities) which would not have been discovered had the research been limited to the study of aggregate firm performance only.

Second, although we considered the relationship between IT and competitive advantage in broad and general terms, the focus of our empirical studies was small firms. Small firms remain a valuable but under-researched area of competitive strategy and, as previously discussed, provide a unique opportunity to test and develop RBV theory. Third, we moved beyond quantitative studies of the relationship between IT and competitive advantage, to investigate the development of dynamic capabilities using interpretive methods. We contend that both quantitative and qualitative studies are important as they measure different aspect of the phenomenon being studied, and can be accommodated in a single mixed methods approach.

Finally, our overall approach was underpinned by solid economic and management theory. That is, we introduced (in Chapter 2) the economic theory of Joseph Schumpeter to explain strategy formulation at the firm level, reviewed the strategic management literature using this theory as a critical lens, and then sought to interpret empirical data (our own and that of other researchers) from this theoretical perspective. Even when we moved beyond this theory in our study of dynamic capability enactment (in Chapter 5), Schumpeter's theory provided the context and we returned to it in our assessment of the results and their implications.

Although this book is not aimed primarily at practising managers, we offer some insights into how theory might inform practice. Economic theory and empirical research suggest that IT *per se* cannot be a source of sustainable competitive advantage but may contribute to such advantage indirectly as a complementary strategic asset. Therefore managers should not dismiss all IT as a commodity or utility factor of production. On the contrary there is increasing evidence that even as the 'raw material' of IT becomes more commoditised, the 'finished goods' of IT is becoming more strategically important.

The importance of viewing IT as an endogenous factor of production, as opposed to an exogenous factor, has been highlighted. If IT is to be used strategically then it will be successful only where the heterogeneous, locally embedded (and therefore hard to copy) character of this strategic asset is recognised and exploited. This means appreciating the interdependencies of IT, business resources and dynamic capabilities. This is the first step in managing IT for competitive advantage.

The book has been concerned to identify and explain the differences between a Ricardian approach to management and a Schumpeterian approach, and in this final chapter we have taken innovation to be a point of departure between the two paradigms. Managers may do well to consider the differences between innovation applied during periods of relative equilibrium and innovation applied during periods of disequilibrium or disruption. In these differences may lie important lessons on how to use IT strategically.

We began this text by asking 'Does IT matter?' We conclude the text by answering with a resounding 'yes!' As Brown and Hagel (2003: 110) say, 'many executives have started to view IT as a commodity because they have not thought aggressively enough about how IT can bring about new business practices. The differentiation is not in IT itself but in the new practices it enables. IT does indeed matter'.

Appendices

Appendix 1

A.4.1 Survey questionnaire

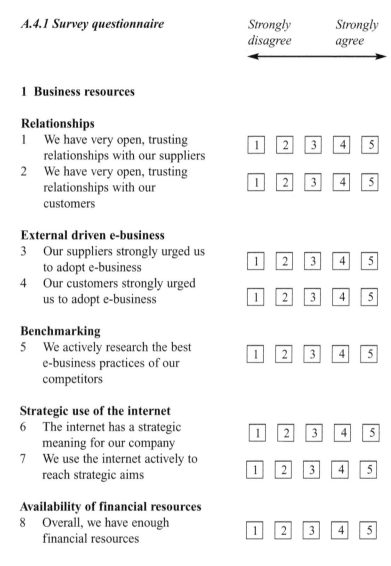

Strongly disagree ← → Strongly agree

1 Business resources

Relationships
1   We have very open, trusting relationships with our suppliers   1 2 3 4 5
2   We have very open, trusting relationships with our customers   1 2 3 4 5

External driven e-business
3   Our suppliers strongly urged us to adopt e-business   1 2 3 4 5
4   Our customers strongly urged us to adopt e-business   1 2 3 4 5

Benchmarking
5   We actively research the best e-business practices of our competitors   1 2 3 4 5

Strategic use of the internet
6   The internet has a strategic meaning for our company   1 2 3 4 5
7   We use the internet actively to reach strategic aims   1 2 3 4 5

Availability of financial resources
8   Overall, we have enough financial resources   1 2 3 4 5

2   IT assets

<table>
<tr><td></td><td colspan="2">*Strongly
disagree*</td><td></td><td colspan="2">*Strongly
agree*</td></tr>
</table>

IT knowledge

 9   Overall, our technical support staff is knowledgeable, when it comes to computer-based systems
│ 1 │ │ 2 │ │ 3 │ │ 4 │ │ 5 │

10   Our firm possesses a high degree of computer-based technical expertise
│ 1 │ │ 2 │ │ 3 │ │ 4 │ │ 5 │

11   We are very knowledgeable about new computer-based innovations
│ 1 │ │ 2 │ │ 3 │ │ 4 │ │ 5 │

12   We have the knowledge to develop and maintain computer-based communication links with our customers
│ 1 │ │ 2 │ │ 3 │ │ 4 │ │ 5 │

IT operations

13   Our firm is skilled at collecting and analysing market information about our customers via computer-based systems
│ 1 │ │ 2 │ │ 3 │ │ 4 │ │ 5 │

14   We routinely utilise computer-based systems to access market information from outside databases
│ 1 │ │ 2 │ │ 3 │ │ 4 │ │ 5 │

15   We have set procedures for collecting customer information from online sources
│ 1 │ │ 2 │ │ 3 │ │ 4 │ │ 5 │

16   We use computer-based systems to analyse customer and market information
│ 1 │ │ 2 │ │ 3 │ │ 4 │ │ 5 │

17   We utilise decision-support systems frequently when it comes to managing customer information
│ 1 │ │ 2 │ │ 3 │ │ 4 │ │ 5 │

18   We rely on computer-based systems to acquire, store, and process information about our customers
│ 1 │ │ 2 │ │ 3 │ │ 4 │ │ 5 │

IT objects

19   Every year we budget a significant amount of funds for new information technology hardware and software
│ 1 │ │ 2 │ │ 3 │ │ 4 │ │ 5 │

20   Our firm creates customised software applications when the need arises
│ 1 │ │ 2 │ │ 3 │ │ 4 │ │ 5 │

21   Our firm's members are linked by a computer network
│ 1 │ │ 2 │ │ 3 │ │ 4 │ │ 5 │

3 Dynamic capabilities	*Strongly disagree*		*Strongly agree*	

Integration

22 Overall, our management has expertise to conduct the major strategic moves
`[1] [2] [3] [4] [5]`

23 Overall, our employees have very good communication skills
`[1] [2] [3] [4] [5]`

24 Our management has expertise in coordinating internal processes and operations
`[1] [2] [3] [4] [5]`

25 The feedback of our customers helps us to improve our products and/or services
`[1] [2] [3] [4] [5]`

26 The internet has changed our processes significantly
`[1] [2] [3] [4] [5]`

27 We have had problems integrating e-business applications in previous IT (reversed)
`[1] [2] [3] [4] [5]`

Learning

28 Overall, our company acquires new knowledge effectively
`[1] [2] [3] [4] [5]`

29 Overall, our company reacts quickly to market changes
`[1] [2] [3] [4] [5]`

30 Overall, our company accumulates knowledge effectively
`[1] [2] [3] [4] [5]`

31 Our company recognises how customers can benefit from new technologies
`[1] [2] [3] [4] [5]`

Reconfiguration

32 We continuously adapt to customers' shifting needs.
`[1] [2] [3] [4] [5]`

33 We quickly respond to competitive strategic moves
`[1] [2] [3] [4] [5]`

34 We easily get rid of assets that have no more value
`[1] [2] [3] [4] [5]`

4 Performance

Internet performance

35 The internet has dramatically increased our productivity

⬚1 ⬚2 ⬚3 ⬚4 ⬚5

36 The internet has improved our competitive position

⬚1 ⬚2 ⬚3 ⬚4 ⬚5

37 The internet has dramatically increased our sales

⬚1 ⬚2 ⬚3 ⬚4 ⬚5

38 The internet has dramatically increased our profitability

⬚1 ⬚2 ⬚3 ⬚4 ⬚5

39 The internet has dramatically improved our overall performance

⬚1 ⬚2 ⬚3 ⬚4 ⬚5

Financial performance

40 Over the past three years, our revenues have been outstanding

⬚1 ⬚2 ⬚3 ⬚4 ⬚5

41 Over the past three years, our revenues have exceeded our competitors'

⬚1 ⬚2 ⬚3 ⬚4 ⬚5

42 Over the past three years, our sales growth has been outstanding

⬚1 ⬚2 ⬚3 ⬚4 ⬚5

43 Over the past three years, our sales growth has exceeded our competitors'

⬚1 ⬚2 ⬚3 ⬚4 ⬚5

44 Over the past three years, our return on assets has been outstanding

⬚1 ⬚2 ⬚3 ⬚4 ⬚5

45 Over the past three years, our return on assets has exceeded our competitors'

⬚1 ⬚2 ⬚3 ⬚4 ⬚5

General questions

46 How many full-time employees
work in your company?

47 What percentage of your revenue is
created by e-commerce?

48 What percentage of the goods and
services you buy are ordered via
the internet?

49 What is your SIC-code?

50 Are you a for-profit or a non-profit
organisation?

For-profit ☐   Non-profit ☐

51 Is your company independent?
(This means you have e.g. no
parent company or you are not part
of a franchising system.)

Yes ☐   No ☐

A.4.2 Correlations

	relation	externdr	benchma	stratint	finre	integr	learning	reconfig	itknow	itops	itobjects	br	dc	it	intperf	fin perf
relation	1.000															
externdr	0.203*	1.000														
benchma	0.109	0.484***	1.000													
stratint	0.198*	0.409***	0.550***	1.000												
finre	0.084	0.179*	0.076	-0.027	1.000											
integr	0.320***	0.278***	0.304***	0.508***	0.246**	1.000										
learning	0.369***	0.294***	0.380***	0.462***	0.276***	0.787***	1.000									
reconfig	0.365***	0.182*	0.129	0.129	0.429***	0.487***	0.520***	1.000								
itknow	0.162	0.255*	0.402***	0.449***	0.154	0.585***	0.543***	0.310***	1.000							
itops	0.041	0.339***	0.547***	0.413***	0.172*	0.468***	0.484***	0.271***	0.512***	1.000						
itobjects	0.008	0.169*	0.318***	0.319***	0.192*	0.399***	0.286***	0.219**	0.622***	0.581***	1.000					
br	0.408***	0.735***	0.768***	0.716***	0.436***	0.529***	0.567***	0.373***	0.474***	0.523***	0.355***	1.000				
dc	0.411***	0.295***	0.322***	0.430***	0.369***	0.880***	0.910***	0.776***	0.560***	0.479***	0.348***	0.575***	1.000			
it	0.088	0.301***	0.497***	0.470***	0.208*	0.578***	0.523***	0.315***	0.855***	0.810***	0.870***	0.535***	0.551***	1.000		
intperf	0.164*	0.429***	0.573***	0.658***	0.071	0.511***	0.510***	0.195*	0.477***	0.496***	0.365***	0.637***	0.476***	0.529***	1.000	
fimperf	0.066	0.171*	0.136	0.044	0.514***	0.274***	0.325***	0.378***	0.162	0.246**	0.143	0.309***	0.381***	0.217**	0.214**	1.000

*	Correlation is significant at the 0.05 level (2-tailed).
**	Correlation is significant at the 0.01 level (2-tailed).
***	Correlation is significant at the 0.001 level (2-tailed).

Appendix 2

A.5.1 Questions used in the interviews with owner-managers

[Introduction]

- Tell me something about your company.
- What is the structure of your organisation?

[Identifying valuable capabilities]
- Why do customers come to your company instead of going to your competitors?
- What makes your product or service special?
- What are valuable capabilities or skills of your company?

[Integration]
- Do you integrate customer feedback inside your company?
- Do you have partnerships with other companies?
- Are you good in using the internet?
- Do you have good team-work in your company?

[Learning]
- Is your company good at generating new ideas with impact?
- Are you good at developing new products, services and process?
- Does your company learn easily?
- Are you involved in any training programmes?

[Reconfiguration]
- Did you have a lot of change inside your company in the past years
- Can you make important changes rapidly?
- Did you change your business processes in the past years?

A.5.2   Sample extract from a coded interview

In this excerpt from the interview (with High Retailer 2) I stands for interviewer (the researcher) and R for the respondent (the owner-manager). The left column shows the codes that emerged during data collection and the right column the codes that were created before data collection. The superscripts are placed at the end of each sentence or section that was linked to the codes.

Manager's activity and commitment	Question and answer	Dynamic capabilities
[A] Com-bui: The manager appears to be committed towards learning. [B] Act-bui: Saying that she couldn't stop learning indicates that she already learns.	I: Does your company learn easily? R: Yes, but I think in this competitive market, you have to keep learning all of the time. [A]I mean if you stop learning then you become complacent and someone else pips you at the post and I think it's what makes us hungry for the industry. [B]You must always be a step ahead and try and find out what is next to come aboard and learn that if need be so yes, I do think so.[1]	[1]Bui-hr: The manager believed that she created competitive advantage by learning and enhancing human resources.

Notes

1   Introduction

1   Carr (2003a: 41) refers to a study by the US Department of Commerce's Bureau of Economic Analysis which finds that whereas in 1965 less than 5 per cent of the capital expenditures of American companies went into information technology, by the early 1980s (after the introduction of the personal computer) this had risen to 15 per cent; by the early 1990s to more than 30 per cent, and by the end of that decade to nearly 50 per cent. He notes that 'even with the recent sluggishness in technology spending, businesses around the world continue to spend well over $2 trillion a year on IT'.

2   Specifically this point centres on the concept of complementarity defined by Powell and Dent-Micallef (1997: 394) as 'the enhancement of resource value, and arises when a resource produces greater returns in the presence of another resource than it does alone'. The concept of complementarity is introduced in Chapter 3 and discussed fully, as well as being empirically tested, in Chapter 4.

3   This excludes short-term declines in productivity due to initial learning effects. Such productivity dips nearly always occur when new technology is introduced and are to be distinguished from longer-term declines in productivity that occur beyond the designated period of technology introduction and implementation.

4   They cite the 2001 McKiney Global Institute study on 'US Productivity Growth, 1995–2000) which they claim was 'the first disciplined attempt to look at the correlation between IT investments and productivity by industry sector'. This study found a significant positive correlation between IT investments and productivity in only six out of 59 industries. The other 53 sectors, accounting for 70 per cent of the economy, saw negligible productivity improvements as a result of their investments in IT.

5   An Application Service Provider (ASP) is an agent or vendor who assembles the functions needed by enterprises (e.g. email, word processing, accounting) and packages them with outsourced development, operation, maintenance and other services, using remote hosting servers across the internet (Austin, 2002).

6   XML, eXtensible Markup Language is the industry standard for representing data on a web services platform.
7   The technological development of Web services and the Semantic Web are beyond the scope of this discussion, but it is interesting to note the extent to which such developments are being applied in different fields. For example, Heiwy (2006) re-uses existing resources and applies new resources to build a Learning Object Repository, based upon standard metadata. Other researchers are concerned that Knowledge Management ontologies are 'properly integrated into existing ontological bases, for the practical purpose of providing the required support for the development of intelligent applications' (Sicilia *et al.*, 2005: 1).
8   Carr (2005: 71) describes Virtualisation as a process or function which 'erases the differences between proprietary computing platforms, enabling applications designed to run on one operating system to be deployed elsewhere' and Grid Computing as an architecture that 'allows large numbers of hardware components, such as servers or disk drives, to effectively act as a single device, pooling their capacity and allocating it automatically to different jobs'.
9   Although the middle layer of the web services architecture (see Ratnasingam, 2004: 385, adapted from Hagel and Brown, 2001) provides specific utilities for resource knowledge management (including directories, brokers, registries, repositories and data transformation) and these utilities can be used (*inter alia*) at the operational level to integrate existing systems within an organisation's Web service application, to create intranets/extranets that provide the right information in an appropriate format and to enable business partners to interact seamlessly (Ratnasingam, 2004: 384), it is unlikely that this is where the greatest benefit will be realised.
10 Jobber (1998) has defined a service as 'any act or performance that one party can offer to another that is essentially intangible and does not result in the ownership of anything. Its production may or may not be tied to a physical product.' Elfatatry and Layzell (2004: 104) observe that 'the essence of this definition is that the main interest in a service is its output, not the means by which the output is generated. This implies that the means of producing the service may change as long as the received output is satisfactory'. So a service is a process or activity which accepts an input, performs some operation on it, thereby adding value, and produces an output. In this sense a service is also a capability. This capability, whether internally or externally generated, needs to be developed, maintained and (periodically) enhanced. In this sense, then, a web service, and the associated service oriented architecture, is much more than hardware, software and data, and more closely approximates to a resource bundle as understood in the RBV.
11 That is, each web service may be called by many applications, and each application may be served by many web services. Note that these relationships exist irrespective of the intention to avoid duplication and redundancy in the provision of services. Good design and management minimises the number of relationships but the final number will always be a function of the number of included applications and services.

12   Typically as SaaS – Software as a Service. Gartner (3 October 2006) has estimated that 25 per cent of all new business software will be delivered in this way by 2011 (http://www.gartner.com.it/page.jsp?id=496886). SaaS is hosted software based on a single set of common code and data definitions that are consumed in a one-to-many model by all contracted customers, at any time, on a pay-for-use basis, or as a subscription based on usage metrics.

13   This point can be considered further through analogy with electricity. Of course, we do not regard the use and management of electricity to be a source of competitive advantage for firms. Electricity is after all a true utility service. But firms can and do use electricity for very different purposes. There are many applications for electrical power, most of which we take for granted. But some applications can and do make a real difference to firm performance. For example, a small manufacturing firm can use electrical power to drive machine tools used to produce finished products that are of superior quality and lower cost than those produced by rival companies. Clearly, as Carr would readily point out, the electricity is not the differentiating factor. This has the same quality and availability for all firms. But we stress the use to which that electricity is put, and the efficiency and effectiveness in managing that use as a source of differentiation. It is the same with IT. The technology alone cannot be a source of competitive advantage but the use and management of that technology (which is crucially dependent on firm resources and capabilities) can.

14   Elsewhere (Schlemmer and Webb, 2006) we use the disaggregated variable of 'internet performance' defined as the degree to which the firm's performance has been improved by the internet. As discussed, this enabled us to evaluate the impact of the internet on other strategic assets and to discover relationships that would not have apparent had we measured only aggregated financial performance.

15   The important point here is that we are able to reject Newbert's (and Powell's) uncoupling of competitive advantage and firm performance as an argument against using financial performance as a measure of competitive advantage while simultaneously accepting that disaggregated measures of firm performance and competitive advantage have also an important part to play.

16   The Profit Impact of Market Strategy (PIMS) database has been used since the early 1970s to predict competitive advantage. It comprises key performance inputs from thousands of affiliated companies across the world. These are analysed to benchmark firm performance and to identify successful strategies. The PIMS database has endured despite being criticised for being too reliant on data from large manufacturing companies, and for confusing correlation with causation in the analysis of competitive advantage.

17   Small Medium (Sized) Enterprises (SMEs), as defined by the European Union, are organisations employing fewer than 250 people. Ninety-nine per cent of all companies in the US and Europe are SMEs (Adam *et al.*, 1998) and they create about 80 per cent of economic growth (Jutla *et al.*, 2002). In the UK there are more than three million of them and yet research on SMEs is still rare, especially in the context of the Internet.

18 So for example, even as we read of yet another IT disaster the IS academic community is engaged in an exercise of intellectual navel gazing, questioning the value of its theories, concept and methods, and even its legitimacy as a discipline. See for example several articles published in the *Communications of the Association for Information Systems*, 2005, volume 12.

2   IT and economic theory

1   Economic rents are most closely associated with Ricardo who used the term only in the context of land. So, quasi-rent originally meant 'as if land'; although in practice rents from capital and labour were similar to rents from land, they also differed in important aspects.

2   For example, the consultants Stern, Stewart and Co. had to conduct approximately 40 modifications to the calculation of EVA in order to control for different accounting conventions [http://www.stearnstewart.com].

3   Equilibrium is central to mercantilism (where it applies to the balance of imports and exports); to classical economics (where it applies to prices), to Marxism (wages) and to Keynesianism (income). Even in Schumpeterian economics, often (but incorrectly) seen as a rejection of the concept of equilibrium, it is – as we shall see later – recognised as a condition of short-term economic growth.

4   PCE is a theoretical concept not intended by economists to reflect real life (although some public markets can be said to be very nearly perfectly competitive). It should be regarded as a pure form, a starting point, against which to consider those restrictions on the movements of goods which characterise (and distort) real markets and which (as we shall discuss) create opportunities and threats for the individual firm.

5   Because PCE is a theoretical concept designed to simplify and illuminate the workings of the real economy, certain assumptions are made that one would not expect to hold in practice. In this scenario, for example, no consideration is given to market entry barriers, market share and economies of scale.

6   Unless otherwise stated, all references are to the first editions of Schumpeter's works (e.g. *History of Economic Development* is 1954). However, because Schumpeter's works have had multiple reprints, where a reference is taken from another source which uses a specific edition, then that edition is given. Such references usually include page numbers (e.g. Schumpeter, 1955: 85 refers to the second edition of *History of Economic Analysis*, as used by Winter, 2006).

7   In this sense, then, the cause of the problems Keynes sought to address was not disequilibrium but rather equilibrium itself. During the depression the laws of supply and demand and the circular flow were behaving in ways that were predictable from an economic point of view, though undesirable from a social point of view.

8   Innovation and technology can be seen as the means by which the economy might recover from a slump and by which it might grow beyond its existing capacity. For example, in classical and neo-classical economic theory (including Keynes), growth was restricted by population growth and when

no new labour factors could be brought to production, production could not progress, unless it became more efficient through the use of technology.

9   That Evolutionary economics is closely associated with the Austrian tradition of microeconomics is unsurprising given that Schumpeter was taught at the University of Vienna by two of the best-known pupils (Eugen von Bohm-Bawerk and Friedrich von Wieser) of the founder of the Austrian School (Carl Menger). Schumpeter's intellectual indebtedness to his former tutors is a matter of record: for example, he called Bohm-Bawerk 'the bourgeois Marx'. Less well recorded is the contribution of German economists to the development of evolutionary economics, in particular their preoccupation in the interwar years with the problems of static equilibrium theory (Warriner, 1931: 38).

10   Rosenberg (2000: 14–17) speculates that Schumpeter's 'numerous expressions of filial piety' to Walras were a means to 'floodlight' the importance that Schumpeter attached to innovation and growth (which Walras ignored). Also, as a useful exercise in 'intellectual deck clearing' to establish his own theory.

11   This is ironic given Schumpeter's subsequent relative dismissal of Ricardo in his *History of Economic Analysis*, 1954; and his extensive discussion of, and obvious admiration for, Marx's contribution to economic theory, in his *Capitalism, Socialism and Democracy*, 1950. For example, he said 'Marx saw [the] process of industrial change more clearly and he realised its pivotal importance more fully than any other economist of his time' (1950: 32). However Maneschi (2000) comments that, although Schumpeter was impressed with the depth of Marx's vision, he was less impressed with his theories.

12   Rosenberg (2000: 13–14) questions this logic. He comments that Schumpeter seems to have regarded not only technology as endogenous but consumer habits also; for example, by stating (in various writings) that consumers merely respond to initiatives and innovations of producers. Thus 'consumer tastes were not independently determined but malleable social phenomena shaped by economic forces' (Rosenberg, 2000: 14). This is a position 'emphatically rejected' by most neo-classical economists, and Rosenberg himself believes that here Schumpeter ruins an otherwise good argument through overstatement.

13   Note that this is the opposite to what Warriner has supposed, i.e. that it was his separation of the world into two economic systems – static and dynamic – that required him to view humans in this way. Whatever the causality of the relationship, it is clear that Schumpeter's views of the workings of the economic system in general and his views on the workings of individuals within it are closely associated.

14   In this matter, as in others, Schumpeter changed his mind. In *Theory of Economic Development* (1911) and *Business Cycles* (1939) invention was treated as exogenous but the adoption of the invention was treated as endogenous. In *Capitalism, Socialism and Democracy* (1942) both invention and innovation had become (or were rapidly becoming) institutionalised in large firms, and so effectively the entrepreneurial function was bureaucratised.

15   For resources A and B, the range of complementarity impacts are (1) increased benefit to A, but not to B, (2) increased benefit to B but not to A,

and (3) increased benefit to A and B. As we shall discuss later in the text, combining two or more assets may add no value, or even result in a reduction in value (which is not of course complementarity).

16 But it is also true that Schumpeter did not explicitly rule out the application of his theory in this manner, indeed he specifically admired Walrasian equilibrium, and therefore he can be accused of leaving the door open for some of the misinterpretations and misunderstandings which subsequently appeared in the literature.

17 It is important to recognise that neither Penrose nor Schumpeter rejected the legitimacy of a firm pursuing profits through market power. The attainment of such a position was a conceptual alternative to what they were proposing (though possibly correlated in practice) and certainly played a part – for example by allowing short term protection from competitors- in long term growth.

3   IT and management theory

1 As we shall see, commonality between DC and RBV leads many researchers to assume that DC is simply an extension of RBV, rooted in the same underlying economic theory of Schumpeterian disequilibrium. We reject this assumption. RBV and DC share a common provenance (in Penrose, 1959) but differ fundamentally in their interpretation of different theories of economic competition at firm level.

2 When considered in relation to strategy, economics may be said to have come full circle. Originating in Adam Smith's concern with the microeconomics of the small firm, the field quickly developed into a concern for the firm as it operated in markets (where price and not the individual entrepreneur acted as the coordinating mechanism). Even in classical (Ricardian) and neo-classical economics ostensibly predicated on firm specific resources, the activities of the firm as a price decision maker also necessitated a consideration of the short-run behaviour of markets. In the IO tradition the firm played a subservient role to industry as the unit of analysis. However, under RBV the firm once more returns to centre stage. In evolutionary economics (neo-Schumpeterian or Austrian School); transaction cost economics and institutional economics the role of the firm as critical unit of analysis is re-confirmed. These changes have necessitated a change in strategising from entrepreneur to manager and back to entrepreneur.

3 In public discourse risk and uncertainty are often regarded as symbiotic and the two terms are used interchangeably. For example, we are told that businesses are managing uncertainty when in fact they can only ever manage risk. This is similar to the popular misconception of time management. As Oshagbemi (1999) has reminded us, managers cannot manage time, managers can only manage *their use* of time.

4 Ironically, Mathews himself can be accused of confusing Ricardian rents (derived from firm resources) and monopoly rents (derived from market positioning). For example, he writes that 'Samsung is even harder to fit with the prevailing rent seeking approaches, as it had neither resources to earn Ricardian rents, nor market position to earn monopoly rents' (2006: 98). As we have seen in the previous chapter, no such distinction can be

made in Ricardian theory because a firm must already be in possession of certain resources in order to be able to identify and benefit from market positioning. Against this it can be said that although Ricardian rents and Monopoly rents are both earned under equilibrium, they differ in their source. Ricardian rents are earned from resources that are in fixed or limited supply. While monopoly rents stem from collusion or government protection (see footnote of Amit and Schoemaker, 1992: 34).

5   As explained in Chapter 2, Schumpeter was not concerned with exogenous change but sought to explain economic growth as a phenomenon of *endogenous* change.

6   Note that here we are talking about the act itself and not its evaluation. Of course, both approaches may only be evaluated *ex post*, but whereas the decision to pick a resource is necessarily made before the resource is picked, the development of a capability can only be done once in possession of that capability. However, see below for a general caveat to such thinking.

7   Later (p. 394) Makadok reflects some of the tautology in general treatments of resources and capabilities when he remarks 'capability building can only improve profitability when other resources are actually acquired' (as opposed to resource picking which can improve profitability *ex ante* because even the decision not to acquire a resource may positively improve profitability). However, does not resource picking assume a pre-existing capability to do so? And where does this capability come from? It can be argued that in fact this capability is also a resource, or at least is based upon the resource of management, knowledge and so on. So the search for causality can be pushed further and further back in fundamental (and existential!) questions on the nature of management and human behaviour itself.

8   Although, as we have already discussed in Chapter 2, it may also be simply that we expect too much from IT, too soon, and too often.

9   Rouse and Daellenbach (1999: 488) make the important if somewhat obvious point that secondary data are unlikely to be a source of competitive advantage, since by definition, secondary data are already in the public domain and therefore available to all. They argue that sources of competitive advantage are firm specific and therefore not amenable to study through secondary data analysis. In Chapters 4 we report primary research using statistical methods and in Chapter 5 we report primary research using interpretive research.

4   IT and the creation of Ricardian rents

1   In the Powell and Dent-Micallef study, some questions specifically biased towards large companies were: 'communications are very open between our home office and our stores', 'our people communicate widely, not just with their own departments' and 'we have lots of conflicts between our home office and our stores.'

2   It is often difficult to distinguish between resources and capabilities, and therefore both are called strategic assets. However, learning and building strategic assets may need some further explanation here. Both learning and building strategic assets are associated with the development of new strategic assets. Whereas learning may be related more to the development

of new capabilities or skills (such as marketing capabilities), building strategic assets may be related more to the development of resources (such as building a production facility). However, both learning and the capability to build strategic assets are regarded here as higher order capabilities.

3   Song *et al.* examined joint ventures (JV), which are actually cooperations of separate firms. However 'a JV is considered a separate legal entity or a "firm" in its own right ... therefore ... [strategic assets] are regarded as "firm"-level traits'.

4   Measured as the mean of business resources and human resources.

5   The database was developed by Belfast City Council, N. Ireland, and co-funded by the European Union as a 'first-stop shop' business resource.

6   A test was conducted for non-response bias. The characteristics of early and late respondents were compared. This did not reveal any significant differences, indicating that non-response was not a problem.

7   The VIF values for the construct were between 1.1 and 1.7. The VIF values for the single variables (after dropping variables) were between 1.1 and 1.4.

8   A Type I error occurs when we accept a false hypothesis as true.

5   IT and the creation of Schumpeterian rents

1   This research is consistent with the view, expressed by Teece *et al.* (1997: 509) and already referred to in Chapter 3, that internal technological, organisational and managerial processes will be most important to wealth creation during periods of rapid technological change.

2   Rouse and Daellenbach are not saying here that low- and average-performing companies should not be studied (on the contrary, they later go on to warn against the dangers of selecting only high and low performers) but simply that such firms should not be lumped together with high-performing companies, because – by definition – sources of sustainable competitive advantage may be found only in high-performing companies. Of course, low- and average-performing companies may be used as control groups to investigate the complete or partial absence of such sources of advantage. Indeed, this is what we did in our own research study (Webb and Schlemmer, 2006).

3   It is also worth noting that although the concept of enactment is applied here to the individual manager, the cognitive frameworks of employees are influenced by their interactions with managers. These interactions lead to commonly shared ideas and concepts. These shared belief systems then provide a framework for noticing and interpreting new stimuli and for coordinating appropriate action. Thus individuals in a firm share experience and knowledge and develop consensual 'views of the world' (Wiley, 1988; Bogner and Barr, 2000).

4   That is, because in this study we wanted to examine the development of dynamic capabilities, we used 'human resources' to avoid any tautology in measuring dependent and independent variables.

5   A pilot study strongly indicated that it would be difficult to get owner-managers to talk about a range of business resources. In addition to time constraints, owner-managers were clearly reluctant to talk about financial performance in further detail. Also, compared with other business resources – such as, for example, 'external driven e-business' which

depended heavily on the strategies of individual firms – customer relationships were relatively easy to compare and contrast between firms.

6   Although the Internet is increasingly blurring the boundaries between industries, we sought to compare and contrast high- and low-performing firms within the same industrial sector, at least in the first instance. We recognise that although this approach improves the research's internal validity it limits the research's external validity (or generalisability). In our discussion of the outcomes of this analysis, greater emphasis is given to comparisons between high and low performers within the IT sector, where performance differentials are greatest and which has most resonance for our study of IT and competitive advantage. Nevertheless, we make occasional comparisons within and between the retail sector in order to clarify issues raised in this discussion.

7   At what point does it become prudent or even necessary to take such a risk? Unfortunately for many firms, particularly small firms, the calculation of risk remains a very inexact science. Often firms will act on the basis of inadequate information, or too late, such that the risk is increased, to the extent that a successful outcome becomes hopelessly improbable. Witness the behaviour of many firms in meltdown scenarios when the risks taken become ever more desperate, or by analogy, the behaviour of a gambler on a losing streak who places increasingly large bets in an attempt to recover losses. The behaviour of failing firms in the face of exponential increases in risk remains an under-researched area, though we have many anecdotal case studies, taken for example, from the dot com collapse.

6   Conclusions

1   To recap, we found no direct link between IT assets and financial performance, and inconclusive results when we evaluated the complementarity of IT assets and other strategic assets. However, we did report some complementarity between the Internet and the strategic assets of business resources and dynamic capabilities. We found no evidence of complementarity between the Internet and IT assets which we attributed to an over-investment in IT or simply being too soon to tell, or possibly both.

2   An example of this can be found in the 'credit crunch' of 2007–2008 when many banks on both sides of the Atlantic faced a period of turbulence in the money markets caused by significant exposures resulting from poor lending in (predominantly) sub-prime markets. Some banks got into great difficulties because their management was not able to make the transition from managing in conditions of equilibrium to managing in conditions of disequilibrium. Some commentators attribute this to a lack of experience, when many CEOs were relatively young and lacked experience of managing in different environments, inside and outside their own firm.

3   Again, it should be emphasised that Table 6.1 is a dichotomy of pure types, presented in order to highlight the different assumptions and ontologies underlying each managerial approach. We do not expect to find such a dichotomy in practice. Indeed, we explicitly reject any such dichotomy in Schumpeter's writing and instead emphasise the dualism which is also found there. We believe that it is this dualism, rather than the dichotomy, that will be of most value to researchers and practitioners.

4 In this text we use 'competences' as the plural of 'competence' but acknowledge that the term 'competencies' is also commonly used in the literature, including by many strategic management researchers.

5 This was a retrospective analysis of the same data we used to report our findings in Chapters 4 and 5. Here we simply re-approached the same data using the critical lens of the resilience concept. We were interested to see (a) how the resilience concept applied to small firms and (b) what this concept could tell us (further) about the relationship between IT and competitive advantage. Our results were summarised in the main body of the text (Chapter 6).

6 See Caulkin, Simon 'Toyota's never-to-be-repeated all-star production' *Observer*, 3 December 2007.

References

Abernathy, W.J. and Utterback, J.M. 1978, 'Patterns of industrial innovation', *Technology Review*, vol. 89, no. 7, pp. 41–47.

Adam, N., Dogramaci, O., Gangopadhyray, A. and Yesha, Y. 1998, *Electronic Commerce: Technical, Business, and Legal Issues*, Prentice Hall, Boston, MA.

Adner, R. and Helfat, C. 2003, 'Corporate effects and dynamic managerial capabilities', *Strategic Management Journal*, vol. 24, no. 10, pp. 1011–1025.

Amit, R. and Schoemaker, P.J.H. 1993, 'Strategic assets and organization rent', *Strategic Management Journal*, vol. 14, no. 1, pp. 33–46.

Amit, R. and Zott, C. 2001, 'Value creation in E-business', *Strategic Management Journal*, vol. 22, no. 6–7, pp. 493–520.

Andersen, H.B. and Cantwell, J. 1999, *How firms differ in their types of technological competence, and why it matters*, Discussion Paper edn, ESRC Centre for Research on Innovation and Competition, University of Manchester.

Anderson, D., Howell-Barber, H., Hill, J., Nasir, J., Lawler, J. and Zheng, L., 2005, 'A study of web services projects in the financial services industry', *Information Systems Management*, vol. 22, no. 1, pp. 66–76.

Austin, R. 2002, 'Jamcracker', *Harvard Business School Case Study*, August, no. 9-602-007.

Bagozzi, R.P. and Phillips, L.W. 1982, 'Representing and testing organizational theories: A holistic construal', *Administrative Science Quarterly*, vol. 17, pp. 459–489.

Bagozzi, R.P. and Yi,Y. 1988, 'On the evaluation of structural equation models', *Journal of the Academy of Marketing Science*, vol. 16, no. 1, pp. 33–46.

Bain, J.S. 1968, *Industrial Organization*, Wiley, New York.

Banker, R. and Kauffman, R.J. 1988, 'Strategic contributions of information technology: An empirical study of ATM networks', *Proceedings of the Ninth International Conference on Information Systems*, eds. J.I. DeGross and M.H. Olson, Minneapolis, MN, pp. 141–150.

Barney, J.B. 1986a, 'Strategic factor markets: Expectations, luck, and business strategy', *Management Science*, vol. 32, no. 10, pp. 1231–1241. Banker, R. and Kauffman, R.J. 1991, 'Reuse and productivity in integrated computer-aided software engineering: An empirical study', *MIS Quarterly*, vol. 15, no. 3, pp. 374–401.

Barney, J.B. 1986b, 'Types of competition and the theory of strategy: Towards an integrative framework', *Academy of Management Review*, vol. 11, no. 4, pp. 791–800.

Barney, J.B. 1991, 'Firm resources and sustained competitive advantage', *Journal of Management*, vol. 17, no. 1, pp. 99–120.

Barney, J.B. 2001a, 'Is the resource-based "view" a useful perspective for strategic management? Yes', *Academy of Management Review*, vol. 26, no. 1, pp. 41–56.

Barney, J.B. 2001b, 'Resource-based theories of competitive advantage: A ten-year retrospective on the resource-based view', *Journal of Management*, vol. 27, no. 6, pp. 643–650.

Barney, J.B. and Arikan, A.M. 2001, 'The resource-based view: Origins and implications' in *The Blackwell Handbook of Strategic Management*, eds. M.A. Hitt, R.E. Freeman and J.S. Harrison, Blackwell, Oxford, pp. 124–188.

Barney, J.B. and Mackey, T.B. 2005, 'Testing resource-based theory' in *Research Methodology in Strategy and Management*, eds. D.J. Ketchen and D.D. Bergh, Elsevier, Greenwich, CT, pp. 1–13.

Barney, J.B. and Wright, P.M. 1998, 'On becoming a strategic partner: The role of human resources in gaining competitive advantage', *Human Resource Management*, vol. 37, pp. 31–46.

BarNir, A., Gallaugher, J. and Auger, P. 2003, 'Business process digitization, strategy, and the impact of firm age and size: The case of the magazine publishing industry', *Journal of Business Venturing*, vol. 18, no. 6, pp. 789–814.

Barua, A., Konana, P., Whinston, A. and Yin, F. 2004, 'An empirical investigation of net-enabled business value', *MIS Quarterly*, vol. 28, no. 4, pp. 585–620.

Benjamin, R. and Levinson, E. 1993, 'A framework for managing IT-enabled change', *Sloan Management Review*, vol. 34, no. 4, pp. 23–33.

Benson, J.K. 1974, 'Comment on Price's *The study of organizational effectiveness*', *Sociological Quarterly*, vol. 14, pp. 273–276.

Bharadwaj, A.S. 2000, 'A resource-based perspective on information technology capability and firm performance: An empirical investigation', *MIS Quarterly*, vol. 24, no. 1, pp. 169–196.

Black, J.A. and Boal, K.B. 1994, 'Strategic resources: Traits, configurations and paths to sustainable competitive advantage', *Strategic Management Journal*, vol. 15, special issue, pp. 141–148.

Bogner, W. and Barr, P. 2000, 'Making sense in hypercompetitive environments', *Organization Science*, vol. 11, no. 2, pp. 212–226.

Boone, C., DeBrabander, B. and Hellemans, J. 2000, 'Research note: CEO locus of control and small firm performance', *Organisation Studies*, vol. 21, no. 3, pp. 641–646.

Brown, B. and Perry, S. 1994, 'Removing the financial performance halo from fortune's "most admired" companies', *The Academy of Management Journal*, vol. 37, no. 5, pp. 1347–1359.

Brown, J. and Hagel, J. 2003, 'Does IT matter?', *Harvard Business Review*, July, pp. 109–112.

Brynjolfsson, E. 1993, 'The productivity paradox of information technology: Review and assessment', Center for Coordination Science, MIT Sloan School of Management, Cambridge, MA.

Brynjolfsson, E. and Hitt, L. 2000, 'Beyond computation: Information technology, organizational transformation and business performance', *The Journal of Economic Perspectives*, vol. 14, no. 4, pp. 23–48.

Burgelman, R.A. 1994, 'Fading memories: A process theory of strategic exit in dynamic environments', *Administrative Science Quarterly*, vol. 39, no. 1, pp. 24–56.

Byrd, T. and Marshall, T. 1997, 'Relating information technology investment to organizational performance: A causal model analysis', *Omega*, vol. 25, no. 1, pp. 43–56.

Caldeira, M. and Ward, J. 2003, 'Using resource-based theory to interpret the successful adoption and use of information systems and technology in manufacturing small and medium-sized enterprises', *European Journal of Information Systems*, vol. 12, no. 2, pp. 127–141.

Caloghirou, Y., Protogerou, A., Spanos, Y. and Papagiannakis, L. 2004, 'Industry- versus firm-specific effects on performance: Contrasting SMEs and large-sized firms', *European Management Journal*, vol. 22, no. 2, pp. 231–243.

Cameron, K.S. and Whetten, D.A. 1983, 'Some conclusions about organizational effectiveness' in *Organizational Effectiveness: A Comparison of Multiple Models*, eds. K.S. Cameron and D.A. Whetten, Academic Press, New York, pp. 261–277.

Cantwell, J. 2000, *Innovation, Profits and Growth: Schumpeter and Penrose (Working Paper)*, University of Reading, UK.

Cantwell, J. 2002, 'Innovation, profits and growth: Penrose and Schumpeter' in *The Growth of the Firm: The Legacy of Edith Penrose*, eds. E.T. Penrose and C. Pitelos, Oxford University Press, Oxford, pp. 215–248.

Cantwell, J. and Andersen, H.B. 1996, 'A statistical analysis of corporate technological leadership historically', *Economics of Innovation and New Technology*, vol. 4, pp. 211–234.

Cantwell, J. and Barrera, M.P. 1998, 'The localisation of corporate technological trajectories in the interwar cartels: Cooperative learning versus an exchange of knowledge', *Economics of Innovation and New Technology*, vol. 6, pp. 257–290.

Cantwell, J. and Fai, F.M. 1999, 'Firms as the source of innovation and growth: The evolution of technological competence', *Journal of Evolutionary Economics*, vol. 9, pp. 331–366.

Capron, L. and Pistre, N. 2002, 'When do acquirers earn abnormal returns?', *Strategic Management Journal*, vol. 23, no. 9, pp. 781–794.

Carmeli, A. and Tishler, A. 2004, 'The relationships between intangible organizational elements and organizational performance', *Strategic Management Journal*, vol. 25, no. 13, pp. 1257–1278.

Carr, N. 2003a, 'IT doesn't matter', *Harvard Business Review*, May, pp. 41–49.

Carr, N. 2003b, 'Does IT matter?', *Harvard Business Review*, July, p. 112.

Carr, N. 2004, *Does IT Matter?* Harvard Business School, Cambridge, MA.

Carr, N. 2005, 'The end of corporate computing', *Sloan Management Review*, vol. 46, no. 3, pp. 67–73.

Carrol, C. and Larkin, C. 1992, 'Executive information technology: A strategic necessity at Motorola codex', *Information Systems Management*, vol. 9, no. 3, pp. 21–29.

Carter, N., Stearns, T., Reynolds, P. and Miller, B. 1994, 'New venture strategies: Theory development within an empirical base', *Strategic Management Journal*, vol. 15, no. 1, pp. 21–41.

Chakravarthy, B. 1986, 'Measuring strategic performance', *Strategic Management Journal*, vol. 7, no. 5, pp. 437–458.

Chakravarthy, B.S. and Lorange, P. 1984, 'Managing strategic adaptation: Options in administrative systems design', *Interfaces*, vol. 14, no. 1, pp. 34–46.

Chan, Y., Bhargava, N. and Street, C. 2006, 'Having arrived: The homogeneity of high-growth small firms', *Journal of Small Business Management*, vol. 44, no. 3, pp. 426–440.

Chaston, I., Badger, B., Mangles, T. and Sadler-Smith, E. 2001, 'The internet and e-commerce: An opportunity to examine organizational learning in progress in small manufacturing firms?', *International Small Business Journal*, vol. 19, no. 2, pp. 13–31.

Chattopadhyay, P., Glick, W. and Huber, G. 2001, 'Organizational actions in response to threats and opportunities', *Academy of Management Journal*, vol. 44, no. 5, pp. 937–955.

Chen, M. and Hambrick, D. 1995, 'Speed, stealth, and selective attack: How small firms differ from large firms in competitive behavior', *Academy of Management Journal*, vol. 38, no. 2, pp. 453–482.

Chen, Y. 2000, 'Building global information systems capabilities: A resource-based approach', *Proceedings of the 2000 information resources management association international conference on challenges of information technology management in the 21st century*, Hershey, PA. pp. 815–818.

Chow, C., Haddad, K. and Williamson, J. 1997, 'Applying the Balanced Scorecard to small companies', *Strategic Finance*, vol. 79, no. 2, pp. 21–28.

Chung, S., Singh, H. and Lee, K. 2000, 'Complementarity, status similarity and social capital as drivers of alliance formation', *Strategic Management Journal*, vol. 21, no. 1, pp. 1–22.

Clark, K.B. and Fujimoto, T. 1991, *Product Development Performance: Strategy, Organization, and Management in the World Auto Industry*, Harvard Business School Press, Cambridge, MA.

Clemence, R.V. 1951, *Essays of Economic Topics of J. A. Schumpeter*, Kennikat Press, Port Washington, NY.

Clemons, E. and Kimbrough, S.O. 1986, 'Information systems, tele-communications, and their effects on industrial organization', *Proceedings of the Seventh International Conference on Information Systems*, San Diego, CA.

Clemons, E. and Row, M. 1988, 'Cash management accounts: A case study in strategic information systems', *Proceedings of the 21st Hawaii International Conference on System Sciences,* IEEE Computer Society Press, Los Alamitos, CA.

Clemons, E. and Row, M. 1991, 'Sustaining IT advantage: The role of structural differences', *MIS Quarterly*, vol. 15, no. 3, pp. 275–292.

Clemons, E. and Weber, B. 1990, 'London's big bang: A case study on information technology, competitive impact, and organizational change', *Journal of Management Information Systems*, vol. 6, no. 4, pp. 41–60.

Cohen, W.M. and Levinthal, D.A. 1989, 'Innovation and learning: The two faces of RandD', *Economic Journal*, vol. 99, pp. 569–596.

Collis, D.J. and Montgomery, C.A. 1995, 'Competing on resources', *Harvard Business Review*, vol. 73, no. 4, pp. 118–128.

Cooper, A.C. 1993, 'Challenges in predicting new venture performance', *Journal of Business Venturing*, vol. 8, no. 3, pp. 231–253.

Copeland, D. and McKenney, J. 1988, 'Airline reservation systems: Lessons from history', *MIS Quarterly*, vol. 12, no. 3, pp. 353–370.

Cousins, P. and Spekman, R. 2003, 'Strategic supply and the management of inter- and intra-organisational relationships', *Journal of Purchasing and Supply Management*, vol. 9, pp. 19–29.

Covin, J.G. and Slevin, D.P. 1990, 'New venture strategic posture, structure, and performance: An industry life cycle analysis', *Journal of Business Venturing*, vol. 5, no. 2, pp. 123–135.

Curley, M. 2004, *Managing Information Technology for Business Value*, Intel Press, Hillsboro, OR.

Daft, R. and Weick, K. 1984, 'Toward a model of organizations as interpretation systems', *Academy of Management Review*, vol. 9, no. 2, pp. 284–295.

Daniel, E. and Wilson, H. 2003, 'The role of dynamic capabilities in e-business transformation', *European Journal of Information Systems*, vol. 12, no. 4, pp. 282–296.

Danneels, E. 2003, 'Tight–loose coupling with customers: The enactment of customer orientation', *Strategic Management Journal*, vol. 24, no. 6, pp. 559–576.

D'Aveni, R.A. 1994, *Hypercompetition: Managing the Dynamics of Strategic Maneuvering*, Free Press, New York.

Davies, N.J., Fensel, D. and Richardson, M. 2004, 'The future of web services', *BT Technology Journal*, vol. 22, no. 1, pp. 118–128.

Day, G.S. and Nedungadi, P. 1994, 'Managerial representations of competitive advantage', *Journal of Marketing*, vol. 58, no. 2, pp. 31–44.

De Vecchi, N. 1995, *Entrepreneurs, Institutions and Economic Change*, Edward Elgar, Aldershot, UK.

Dean, T., Brown, R. and Bamford, C. 1998, 'Differences in large and small firm responses to environmental context: Strategic implications from a comparative analysis of business formations', *Strategic Management Journal*, vol. 19, no. 8, pp. 709–728.

Dean, T.J. and Meyer, G.D. 1996, 'Industry environments and new venture formations in U.S. manufacturing: A conceptual and empirical analysis of demand determinants', *Journal of Business Venturing*, vol. 11, no. 2, pp. 107–132.

Dedrick, J., Gurbaxani, V. and Kraemer, K. 2003, 'Information technology and economic performance: A critical review of the empirical evidence', *ACM Computing Surveys*, vol. 35, no. 1, pp. 1–28.

Delmas, M. 2002, 'Innovating against European rigidities: Institutional environment and dynamic capabilities', *Journal of High Technology Management Research*, vol. 13, no. 1, pp. 19–43.

DeLone, W. and McLean, E. 2003, 'The DeLone and McLean model of information systems success: A ten-year update', *Journal of Management Information Systems*, vol. 19, no. 4, pp. 9–30.

Dembla, P., Palvia, P., Brooks, L., Krishnan, B. 2004, 'Adoption of web-based services for information search by organisations: A multilevel contextual analysis', *Proceedings of the Northeast Decision Sciences Institute Annual Meeting*, Atlantic City, NJ.

Dess, G. 1987, 'Consensus on strategy formulation and organizational performance: Competitors in a fragmented industry', *Strategic Management Journal*, vol. 8, no. 3, pp. 259–277.

Dess, G. and Robinson, R.J. 1984, 'Measuring organizational performance in the absence of objective measures: The case of the privately-held firm and conglomerate business unit', *Strategic Management Journal*, vol. 5, no. 3, pp. 265–273.

Dierickx, I. and Cool, K. 1989, 'Assets stock accumulation and sustainability of competitive advantage', *Management Science*, vol. 35, no. 12, pp. 1504–1511.

Dosi, G. 1982, 'Technological paradigms and technological trajectories: A suggested interpretation of the determinants and directions of technical change', *Research Policy*, vol. 11, pp. 147–162.

Dougherty, D. 1995, 'Managing your core incompetences for corporate venturing', *Entrepreneurship Theory and Practice*, vol. 19, no. 3, pp. 113–135.

Duh, R.R., Chow, C.W. and Chen, H. 2006, 'Strategy, IT applications for planning and control, and firm performance: The impact of impediments to IT implementation', *Information & Management*, vol. 43, no. 8, pp. 939–949.

Duhan, S., Levy, M. and Powell, P. 2001, 'Information systems strategies in knowledge-based SMEs: The role of core competences', *European Journal of Information Systems*, vol. 10, no. 1, pp. 25–40.

Eisenhardt, K. 1989, 'Making fast strategic decisions in high-velocity environments', *Academy of Management Journal*, vol. 32, no. 3, pp. 543–576.

Eisenhardt, K.M. and Brown, S.L. 1999, 'Patching: Re-stitching business portfolios in dynamic markets', *Harvard Business Review*, vol. 77, no. 3, pp. 72–82.

Eisenhardt, K. and Galunic, D.C. 2000, 'Coevolving: At last a way to make synergies work', *Harvard Business Review*, vol. 78, no. 1, pp. 91–101.

Eisenhardt, K.M. and Martin, J.A. 2000, 'Dynamic capabilities: What are they?', *Strategic Management Journal*, vol. 21, no. 10–11, pp. 1105–1121.

Elfatatry, A. and Layzell, P. 2004, 'Negotiating in service oriented environments', *Communications of the ACM*, vol. 47, no. 8, pp. 103–108.

Ellis, I. and Wagner, B. 2005, 'E-business development: An exploratory investigation of the small firm', *International Small Business Journal*, vol. 23, no. 6, pp. 604–609.

Ethiraj, S., Kale, P., Krishnan, M.S. and Singh, J. 2005, 'Where do capabilities come from and how do they matter? A study in the software services industry', *Strategic Management Journal*, vol. 26, no. 1, pp. 25–45.

Feeny, D.F. and Ives, B. 1990, 'In search of sustainability: Reaping long-term advantage from investments in information technology', *Journal of Management Information Systems*, vol. 7, no. 1, pp. 27–46.

Feeny, D. and Willcocks, L. 1998, 'Re-design the IS function around core capabilities', *Long Range Planning*, vol. 31, no. 3, pp. 354–367.

Feindt, S., Jeffcoate, J. and Chappel, C. 2002, 'Identifying success factors for rapid growth in SME e-commerce', *Small Business Economics*, vol. 19, no. 1, pp. 51–62.

Fillis, I., Johansson, U. and Wagner, B. 2004, 'A qualitative investigation of smaller firm e-business development', *Journal of Small Business and Enterprise Development*, vol. 11, no. 3, pp. 349–361.

Fiol, C.M. 1991, 'Managing culture as a competitive resource: An identity-based view of sustainable competitive advantage', *Journal of Management*, vol. 17, no. 1, pp. 191–211.

Fletcher, P. and Waterhouse, M. 2002, *Web Services Business Strategies and Architectures*, Expert Press, London.

Floyd, S.W. and Woolridge, B. 1990, 'Path analysis of the relationship between competitive strategy, information technology, and financial performance', *Journal of Management Information Systems*, vol. 7, no. 1, pp. 47–64.

Fombrun, C. and Shanley, M. 1990, 'What's in a name? Reputation building and corporate strategy', *Academy of Management Journal*, vol. 33, no. 2, pp. 233–258.

Foong, S.Y. 1999, 'Effect of end-user personal and systems attributes on computer-based information systems success in Malaysian SMEs', *Journal of Small Business Management*, vol. 37, no. 3, pp. 81–87.

Forbes, D. 2005, 'Managerial determinants of decision speed in new ventures', *Strategic Management Journal*, vol. 26, no. 3, pp. 355–366.

Foss, N.J. 1997, 'Resources and strategy: A brief overview of themes and contributions' in *Resources, Firms, and Strategies*, ed. N.J. Foss, Oxford University Press, Oxford, pp. 3–18.

Foss, N.J. 2005, *Strategy, Economic Organization, and the Knowledge Economy: The Coordination of Firms and Resources*, Oxford University Press, Oxford.

Freeman, C. and Perez, C. 1988, 'Structural crises of adjustment, business cycles and investment behaviour' in *Technical Change and Economic Theory*, eds. G. Dosi, R.R. Freeman, G. Nelson, G. Silverberg and L.L.G. Soete, Frances Pinter, London.

Fry, L.W. and Smith, D.A. 1987, 'Congruence, contingency, and theory building', *The Academy of Management Review*, vol. 12, no. 1, pp. 117–132.

Gale, B.T. 1972, 'Market share and rate of return', *Review of Economics and Statistics*, vol. 54, no. 4, pp. 412–423.

Gans, J. and Quiggin, J. 2003, 'A technological and organizational explanation for the size distribution of firms', *Small Business Economics*, vol. 21, no. 3, pp. 243–256.

Garud, R., Kumaraswamy, A. and Sambamurthy, V. 2006, 'Emergent by design: performance and transformation at Infosys Technologies', *Organization Science*, vol. 17, no. 2, pp. 277–290.

Garvin, D. 1988, *Managing Quality*, Free Press, New York.

Geletkanycz, M. 1997, 'The salience of "cultural consequences": The effects of cultural values on top executive commitment to the status quo', *Strategic Management Journal*, vol. 18, no. 8, pp. 615–634.

Gibbert, M. 2006, 'Munchausen, Black Swans, and the RBV: Response to Levitas and Ndofor', *Journal of Management Inquiry*, vol. 15, no. 2, pp. 145.

Gillmor, S. 2002, 'Show me the model', *InfoWorld*, December, no. 9, pp. 66–68.

Gottschalk, K., Graham, S., Kreger, H., and Snell, J., 2002, 'Introduction to web services architecture', *IBM Systems Journal*, vol. 41, no. 2, pp. 170–178.

Granstrand, O. and Sjolander, S. 1990, 'Managing innovation in multi-technology corporations', *Research Policy*, vol. 19, pp. 35–60.

Granstrand, O., Patel, P. and Pavitt, K.L.R. 1997, 'Multi-technology corporations: Why they have disributed rather than distinctive core competencies', *California Management Review*, vol. 39, pp. 8–25.

Grant, R. 1991, 'A resource-based theory of competitive advantage: Implications for strategy formulation', *California Management Review*, vol. 33, no. 3, pp. 114–135.

Grant, R. 1996, 'Toward a knowledge-based theory of the firm', *Strategic Management Journal*, vol. 17, Winter special issue, pp. 109–113.

Grant, R. 1997, 'The knowledge-based view of the firm: Implications and management practice', *Long Range Planning*, vol. 30, no. 3, pp. 450–454.

Gribbins, M. and King, R. 2004, 'Electronic retailing strategies: A case study of small businesses in the gifts and collectibles industry', *Electronic Markets*, vol. 14, no. 2, pp. 138–152.

Gujarati, D. 1995, *Basic Econometrics*, 3rd edn, McGraw-Hill, New York.

Gulati, R. 1999, 'Network location and learning: The influence of network resources and firm capabilities on alliance formation', *Strategic Management Journal*, vol. 20, no. 5, pp. 397–420.

Hagel, J. and Brown, J.S. 2001, 'An overview of web services', *Harvard Business Review*, vol. 79, no. 9, pp. 107–115.

Hall, R. 1993, 'A framework linking intangible resources and capabilities to sustainable competitive advantage', *Strategic Management Journal*, vol. 14, no. 8, pp. 607–618.

Hamel, G. and Valikangas, L. 2003, 'The quest for resilience', *Harvard Business Review*, vol. 81, no. 9, pp. 52–63.

Hameresh, R.G., Anderson, M.J. and Harris, J.E. 1978, 'Strategies for low market share business', *Harvard Business Review*, vol. 56, no. 3, pp. 95–102.

Hannan, M.T. and Freeman, J.H. 1984, 'Structural inertia and organizational change', *American Journal of Sociology*, vol. 89, pp. 149–164.

Hansen, M.T. 1999, 'The search-transfer problem: The role of weak ties in sharing knowledge across organization subunits', *Administrative Science Quarterly*, vol. 44, no. 1, pp. 82–111.

Hargadon, A. and Sutton, R.I. 1997, 'Technology brokering and innovation in a product development firm', *Administrative Science Quarterly*, vol. 42, no. 4, pp. 716–749.

Harrigan, K.R. 1985, *Strategic Flexibility*, Lexington Books, Lexington, MA.

Hatch, N.W. and Dyer, J.H. 2004, 'Human capital and learning as a source of sustainable competitive advantage', *Strategic Managment Journal*, vol. 25, no. 12, pp. 1155–1178.

Hawawini, G., Subramanian, V. and Verdin, P. 2003, 'Is performance driven by industry- or firm-specific factors? New look at the old evidence', *Strategic Management Journal*, vol. 24, no. 1, pp. 1–16.

Heertje, A. 1981, *Schumpeter's Vision: Capitalism, Socialism and Democracy after 40 Years*, Praeger, New York.

Heiwy, V. 2006, 'Using the semantic web for the reuse of learning objects', *International Journal of Knowledge and Learning*, vol. 2, no. 3/4, pp. 263–278.

Helfat, C. 1997, 'Know-how and asset complementarity and dynamic capability accumulation', *Strategic Management Journal*, vol. 18, no. 5, pp. 339–360.

Helfat, C. and Raubitschek, R. 2000, 'Product sequencing: Co-evolution of knowledge, capabilities and products', *Strategic Management Journal*, vol. 21, no. 10/11, pp. 961–979.

Henderson, J.C. and Sifonis, J.G. 1988, 'The value of IS planning: Understanding contingency, validity, and IS markets', *MIS Quarterly*, vol. 12, no. 2, pp. 186–200.

Henderson, J. and Venkatraman, N. 1993, 'Strategic alignment: Leveraging information technology for transforming organizations', *IBM Systems Journal*, vol. 32, no. 1, pp. 4–16.

Henderson, R. 1993, 'Underinvestment and incompetence as responses to radical innovation: Evidence from the photolithographic alignment equipment industry', *Rand Journal of Economics*, vol. 24, no. 2, pp. 248–270.

Henderson, R. and Cockburn, I. 1994, 'Measuring competence? Exploring firm effects in pharmaceutical research', *Strategic Management Journal*, vol. 15, Winter special issue, pp. 63–84.

Hitt, M. and Ireland, R.D. 2002, 'The essence of strategic leadership: Managing human and social capital', *Journal of Leadership and Organizational Studies*, vol. 9, no. 1, pp. 3–14.

Hitt, M.A., Hoskisson, R.E. and Harrison, J.S. 1991, 'Strategic competitiveness in the 1990s: Challenges and opportunities for U.S. executives', *Academy of Management Executive*, vol. 5, no. 2, pp. 7–22.

Hodgkinson, G. 1997, 'The cognitive analysis of competitive structures: A review and critique', *Human Relations*, vol. 50, no. 6, pp. 625–654.

Hodgson, G.M. 1993, *Economics and Evolution*, Polity Press, Cambridge, UK.

Hofer, C.W. 1983, 'Rova: A new measure for assessing organizational performance', *Advance in Strategic Management*, vol. 2, pp. 43–55.

Holland, C., Lockett, G. and Blackman, I. 1992, 'Planning the electronic data interchange', *Strategic Management Journal*, vol. 13, no. 7, pp. 539–550.

House, D. 2004, 'People, power and profits: Linking strategy to business growth', *Handbook of Business Strategy*, vol. 5, no. 1, pp. 257–261.

Hudson, M., Smart, A. and Bourne, M. 2001, 'Theory and practice in SME performance measurement systems', *International Journal of Operations & Production Management*, vol. 21, no. 8, pp. 1096–1115.

Igbaria, M., Zinatelli, N. and Cavaye, A. 1998, 'Analysis of information technology success in small firms in New Zealand', *International Journal of Information Management*, vol. 18, no. 2, pp. 103–119.

Ihlstrom, C. and Nilsson, M. 2003, 'E-business adoption by SMEs: Prerequisites and attitudes of SMEs in a Swedish network', *Journal of Organizational Computing and Electronic Commerce*, vol. 13, no. 3/4, pp. 211–223.

Jelassi, T. and Figon, O. 1994, 'Competing through EDI at Brun Bascot: Achievements in France and ambitions for the single European market', *MIS Quarterly*, vol. 18, no. 4, pp. 337–352.

Jobber, D. 1998, *Principles and Practices of Marketing*, McGraw-Hill, New York.

Johnson, D. and Hoopes, D. 2003, 'Managerial cognition, sunk costs, and the evolution of industry structure', *Strategic Management Journal*, vol. 24, no. 10, pp. 1057–1068.

Johnston, H.R. and Carrico, S.R. 1988, 'Developing capabilities to use information strategically', *MIS Quarterly*, vol. 12, no. 1, pp. 36–48.

Jones, C. 2004, 'An alternative view of small firm adoption', *Journal of Small Business and Enterprise Development*, vol. 11, no. 3, pp. 362–370.

Joshi, P., Singh, H. and Pippen, A.D., 2004, 'Web services: Measuring practitioner attitude', *Internet Research*, vol. 14, no. 5, pp. 366–371.

Jutla, D., Bodoril, P. and Dhaliwal, J. 2002, 'Supporting the e-business readiness of small and medium-sized enterprises: Approaches and metrics', *Internet Research: Electronic Networking Applications and Policy*, vol. 12, no. 2, pp. 139–164.

Jutla, D., Bodorik, P. and Wang, Y. 1999, 'Developing internet e-commerce benchmarks', *Information Systems*, vol. 24, no. 6, pp. 475–493.

Kearns, G.S. 2007, 'How the internal environment impacts information systems project success: An investigation of exploitative and explorative firms', *The Journal of Computer Information Systems*, vol. 48, no. 1, pp. 63–75.

Keen, P. 1993, 'Information technology and the management difference: A fusion map', *IBM Systems Journal*, vol. 32, no. 1, pp. 17–39.

Keller-Johnson, L. 2002, 'New views on digital CRM', *MIT Sloan Management Review*, vol. 44, no. 1, pp. 10–27.

Kettinger, W., Grover, V. and Segars, A. 1995, 'Do strategic systems really pay off?', *Information Systems Management*, vol. 12, no. 1, pp. 35–43.

Kettinger, W., Grover, V., Guha, S. and Segars, A. 1994, 'Strategic information systems revisited: A study in sustainability and performance', *MIS Quarterly*, vol. 18, no. 1, pp. 31–58.

Keynes, J.M. 1936, *The General Theory of Employment Interest and Money*, Macmillan, London.

King, W., Grover, V., Hufnagel, E. 1989, 'Using information and information technology for sustainable competitive advantage', *Information and Management*, vol. 17, no. 2, pp. 87–93.

Kirchoff, B. 1977, 'Organization effectiveness measurement and policy research', *Academy of Management Review*, vol. 2, pp. 347–355.

Kirchoff, B. and Kirchoff, J.J. 1980, 'Empirical assessment of the strategy/tactics dilemma', *Academy of Management Proceedings*, pp. 7–15.

Klassen, R. and Whybark, D.C. 1999, 'The impact of environmental technologies on manufacturing performance', *Academy of Management Journal*, vol. 42, no. 6, pp. 599–615.

Kleindl, B. 2000, 'Competitive dynamics and new business models for SMEs in the virtual market place', *Journal of Developmental Entrepreneurship*, vol. 5, no. 1, pp. 73–85.

Knight, F.H. 1942, 'Profit and entrepreneurial functions', *Journal of Economic History*, vol. 2, pp. 126–132.

Kogot, B. and Zander, U. 1992, 'Knowledge of the firm, combinative capabilities, and the replication of technology.', *Organization Science*, vol. 3, no. 3, pp. 383–397.

Kotha, S., Rindova, V. and Thothaermel, F. 2001, 'Assets and actions: Firm-specific factors on the internationalization of U.S. internet firms', *Journal of International Business Studies*, vol. 32, no. 4, pp. 769–791.

Krishnan, H., Miller, A. and Judge, W. 1997, 'Diversification and top management complementarity: Is performance improved by merging similar or dissimilar teams?', *Strategic Management Journal*, vol. 18, no. 5, pp. 361–374.

Lado, A. and Wilson, M. 1994, 'Human resource systems and sustained competitive advantage: A competency-based perspective', *Academy of Management Review*, vol. 19, no. 4, pp. 699–727.

Lant, T. K., Milliken, F. J. and Batra, B. 1992, 'The role of managerial learning and interpretation in strategic persistence: An empirical exploration', *Strategic Management Journal*, vol. 13, no. 8, pp. 585–608.

Lederer, A. and Sethi, V. 1988, 'The implementation of strategic information systems planning methodologies', *MIS Quarterly*, vol. 12, no. 3, pp. 445–461.

Lee, C., Lee, K. and Pennings, J. 2001, 'Internal capabilities, external networks, and performance: A study on technology-based ventures', *Strategic Management Journal*, vol. 22, no. 6/7, pp. 615–640.

Lee, K., Lim, G. and Tan, S. 1999, 'Dealing with resource disadvantage: Generic strategies for SMEs', *Small Business Economics*, vol. 12, no. 4, pp. 299–311.

Leonard-Barton, D. 1992, 'Core capabilities and core rigidities: A paradox in managing product development', *Strategic Management Journal*, vol. 13, no. 1, pp. 111–125.

Levinthal, D.A. and March, J.G. 1993, 'The myopia of learning', *Strategic Management Journal*, vol. 14, no. 1, pp. 95–112.

Levitas, E. and Ndofor, H.A. 2006, 'What to do with the resource-based view: A few suggestions for what ails the RBV that supporters and opponents might accept', *Journal of Management Inquiry*, vol. 15, no. 2, pp. 135–144.

Levitt, B. and March, J.G. 1988, 'Organizational learning', *Annual Review of Sociology*, vol. 14, pp. 319–340.

Li, M. Ye, L.R. 1999, 'Information technology and firm performance: Linking with environmental, strategic and managerial contexts', *Information and Management*, vol. 35, no. 1, pp. 3–51.

Lim, B. and Wen, H., 2003, 'Web services: An analysis of the technology, its benefits, and implementation difficulties', *Information Systems Journal*, vol. 20, no. 2, pp. 49–58.

Lin, C.Y. 1998, 'Success factors of small and medium-sized enterprises in Taiwan: An analysis of cases', *Journal of Small Business Management*, vol. 36, no. 4, pp. 43–56.

Lindsey, D., Cheney, P., Kasper, G. and Ives, B. 1990, 'TELCOT: An application of information technology for competitive advantage in the cotton industry', *MIS Quarterly*, vol. 14, no. 4, pp. 346–357.

Lippman, S.A. Rumelt, R.P. 1982, 'Uncertain imitability: An analysis of interfirm differences in efficiency under competition', *Bell Journal of Economics*, vol. 13, pp. 418–438.

Lockett, A. and Thompson, S. 2001, 'The resource-based view and economics', *Journal of Management*, vol. 27, no. 6, pp. 723–754.

Lyytinen, K. and Rose, G.M. 2006, 'Information system development agility as organizational learning', *European Journal of Information Systems*, vol. 15, no. 2, pp. 183–199.

McAfee, A. 2005, 'Will web services really transform collaboration?', *Sloan Management Review*, vol. 46, no. 2, pp. 78–84.

McDougall, P.P., Covin, R.B., Robinson, R.B.J. and Herron, L. 1994, 'The effects of industry growth and strategic breadth on new venture performance and strategy content', *Strategic Management Journal*, vol. 15, no. 7, pp. 537–554.

McGregor, D. 1960, *The Human Side of Enterprise*, McGraw-Hill, New York.

McWilliams, A. and Siegel, D. 1997, 'Event studies in management research: Theoretical and empirical issues', *Academy of Management Journal*, vol. 40, no. 3, pp. 626–657.

Maerz, E. 1991, *Joseph Schumpeter: Scholar, teacher and politician*, Yale University Press, New Haven, CN.

Magretta, J. 1998, 'The power of virtual integration: An interview with Dell Computer's Michael Dell', *Harvard Business Review*, vol. 76, no. 2, pp. 72–84.

Mahmood, M. 1993, 'Associating organizational strategic performance with information technology: An exploratory research', *European Journal of Information Systems*, vol. 2, no. 3, pp. 185–200.

Mahmood, M. and Mann, G. 1993, 'Measuring the organizational impact of information technology investment: An exploratory study', *Journal of Information Systems*, vol. 10, no. 1, pp. 97–122.

Mahmood, M. and Soon, S.K. 1991, 'A comprehensive model for measuring the potential impact of information technology on organizational strategic variables', *Decision Sciences*, vol. 22, no. 4, pp. 869–897.

Mahoney, J.T. 1995, 'The management of resources and the resource of management', *Journal of Business Research*, vol. 33, no. 2, pp. 91–101.

Mahoney, J. and Pandian, R. 1992, 'The resource based view within the conversation of strategic management', *Strategic Management Journal*, vol. 13, no. 5, pp. 363–382.

Makadok, R. 2001, 'Toward a synthesis of the resource-based and dynamic-capability views of rent creation', *Strategic Management Journal*, vol. 22, no. 5, pp. 387–401.

Maneschi, A. 2000, 'Schumpeter's "Vision" as a filter for his evaluation of other economists' visions', Working Paper No. 00-W17: Department of Economics, Vanderbilt University, Nashville, TN.

Mann, M., Rudman, R., Jecknes, T. and McNurlin, B. 1991, 'EPRINET: Leveraging knowledge in the electric utility industry', *MIS Quarterly*, vol. 15, no. 3, pp. 402–421.

March, J.G. 1991, 'Exploration and exploitation in organizational learning', *Organization Science*, vol. 2, no. 1, pp. 71–87.

March, J.G. 2006, 'Rationality, foolishness, and adaptive intelligence', *Strategic Management Journal*, vol. 27, no. 3, pp. 201–214.

Marr, B., Schiuma, G. and Neely, A. 2002, 'Assessing strategic knowledge assets in e-business', *International Journal of Business Performance Management*, vol. 4, no. 2/3/4, pp. 279–295.

Martin, L. and Matlay, H., 2003, 'Innovative use of the internet in established small firms: The impact of knowledge management and organizational learning in accessing new opportunities', *Qualitative Market Research*, vol. 6, no. 1, pp. 18–27.

Martinsons, M.G. and Leung, A. 2002, 'Strategic information systems: A success factors model', *International Journal of Services Technology and Management*, vol. 3, no. 4, pp. 398–416.

Mason, E.S. 1939, 'Price and production policies of large scale enterprises', *American Economic Review*, vol. 29, pp. 61–74.

Mata, F.J., Fuerst, W.L. and Barney, J.B. 1995, 'Information technology and sustained competitive advantage: A resource-based analysis', *MIS Quarterly*, vol. 19, no. 4, pp. 487–505.

Mathews, J.A. 2006, 'Ricardian rents or Knightian profits? More on Austrian insights on strategic organization', *Strategic Organization*, vol. 4, no. 1, pp. 97–108.

Melville, N., Kraemer, K. and Gubraxani, V. 2004, 'Review: Information technology and organizational performance: An integrative model of IT business value', *MIS Quarterly*, vol. 28, no. 2, pp. 283–322.

Meroño-Cerdan, A.L. and Soto-Acosta, P. 2007, 'External web content and its influence on organizational performance', *European Journal of Information Systems*, vol. 16, no. 1, pp. 66–80.

Middleton, P. Sutton, J. 2005, *Lean Software Strategies: Proven Techniques for Managers and Developers*, Productivity Press, New York.

Miles, M.B. and Huberman, A.M. 1984, *Qualitative Data Analysis: A Sourcebook of New Methods*, Sage, London.

Milgrom, P. and Roberts, J. 1990, 'The economics of modern manufacturing: Technology, strategy, and organization', *American Economic Review*, vol. 80, no. 3, pp. 511–528.

Miller, D. and Chen, M., 1994, 'Sources and consequences of competitive inertia', *Administrative Science Quarterly*, vol. 39, pp. 1–23.

Miller, D. and Chen, M., 1996, 'The simplicity of competitive repertoires', *Academy of Management Journal*, vol. 17, pp. 419–440.

Mintzberg, H., Raisinghani, D. and Theoret, A. 1976, 'The structure of unstructured decision processes', *Administrative Science Quarterly*, vol. 21, no. 1, pp. 246–275.

Montealegre, R. 2002, 'A process model of capability development: Lessons from the electronic commerce strategy at Bolsa de Valores de Guayaquil', *Organization Science*, vol. 13, no. 5, pp. 514–531.

Mosakowski, E. and McKelvey, B. 1997, 'Predicting rent generation in competence-based competition' in *Competence-Based Strategic Management*, eds. A. Hence and R. Sanchez, Wiley, Chichester, UK, pp. 65–85.

Murphy, G., Trailer, J. and Hill, R. 1996, 'Measuring performance in entrepreneurship research', *Journal of Business Research*, vol. 36, no. 1, pp. 15–23.

Murtaza, M. and Shah, J. R. 2004, 'Managing information for effective business partner relationships', *Information Systems Management*, vol. 12, no. 2, pp. 43–52.

Neirotti, P. and Paolucci, E. 2007, 'Assessing the strategic value of Information Technology: An analysis on the insurance sector', *Information and Management*, vol. 44, no. 6, pp. 568–582.

Nelson, R. and Winter, S. 1982, *An Evolutionary Theory of Economic Change*, Belknap Press, Cambridge, MA.

Neo, B.S. 1988, 'Factors facilitating the use of information technology for competitive advantage: An exploratory study', *Information & Management*, vol. 15, no. 4, pp. 191–201.

Newbert, S.L. 2007, 'Empirical research on the resource-based view of the firm: An assessment and suggestions for future research', *Strategic Management Journal*, vol. 28, no. 2, pp. 121–146.

Ocasio, W. 1997, 'Towards an attention-based view of the firm', *Strategic Management Journal*, vol. 18, no. Summer special issue, pp. 187–206.

Oh, W. and Pinsonneault, A. 2007, 'On the Assessment of the Strategic Value of Information Technologies: Conceptual and Analytical Approaches', *MIS Quarterly*, vol. 31, no. 2, pp. 239–266.

Osborne, J.D., Stubbart, C. and Ramaprasad, A. 2001, 'Strategic groups and competitive enactment: A study of dynamic relationships between mental models and performance', *Strategic Management Journal*, vol. 22, no. 5, pp. 435–454.

Oshagbemi, T. 1999, *Managers and Their Time*, Blackhall Publishing, Dublin.

Pallant, J. 2002, *SPSS Survival Manual*, Open University Press, Buckingham.

Palvia, P. and Palvia, S. 1999, 'An examination of the IT satisfaction of small business users', *Information and Management*, vol. 35, no. 3, pp. 127–137.

Pavitt, K.L.R., Robson, M. and Townsend, J. 1989, 'Technological accumulation, diversification and organisation in UK companies, 1945–1983', *Management Science*, vol. 35, pp. 81–99.

Penrose, E. 1959, *The Theory of Growth of the Firm*, Basil Blackwell, London.

Peteraf, M.A. 1993, 'The cornerstones of competitive advantage: A resource-based view', *Strategic Management Journal*, vol. 14, no. 3, pp. 179–191.

Pettigrew, A. 1985, *The Awakening Giant*, Basil Blackwell, Oxford.

Pollard, C., 2003, 'E-service adoption and use in small farms in Australia: Lessons learned from a government-sponsored programme', *Journal of Global Information Technology Management*, vol. 16, no. 2, pp. 45–57.

Popper, K. 1959, *The Logic of Scientific Discovery*, Hutchinson, London.

Porac, J.F. and Thomas, H. 1990, 'Taxonomy mental models in competitor definition', *Academy of Management Review*, vol. 15, no. 1, pp. 224–240.

Porac, J., Thomas, H. and Baden-Fuller, C. 1989, 'Competitive groups as cognitive communities: The case of Scottish knitwear manufacturers', *Journal of Management Studies*, vol. 26, no. 4, pp. 397–416.

Porter, M. 1980, *Competitive Strategy: Techniques for Analyzing Industries and Competitors*, Free Press, New York.

Porter, M. 1985, *Competitive Advantage: Creating and Sustaining Superior Performance*, Free Press, New York.

Porter, M.E. 1991, 'Towards a dynamic theory of strategy', *Strategic Management Journal*, vol. 12, Winter, pp. 95–117.

Porter, M.E. 2001, 'Strategy and the internet', *Harvard Business Review*, March, pp. 63–78.

Powell, T. 2001, 'Competitive advantage: Logical and philosophical considerations', *Strategic Management Journal*, vol. 22, no. 9, pp. 875–893.

Powell, T.C. and Dent-Micallef, A. 1997, 'Information technology as competitive advantage: The role of human, business, and technology resources', *Strategic Management Journal*, vol. 18, no. 5, pp. 375–405.

Powell, W.W., Koput, K.W. and Smith-Doerr, L. 1996, 'Interorganizational collboration and the locus of innovation', *Administrative Science Quarterly*, vol. 41, no. 1, pp. 116–145.

Prahalad, C.K. and Hamel, G. 1990, 'The core competence of the corporation', *Harvard Business Review*, vol. 68, no. 3, pp. 79–91.

Prendergast, R. 2006, 'Schumpeter, Hegel and the vision of development', *Cambridge Journal of Economics*, vol. 30, no. 2, pp. 253.

Priem, R. and Butler, J. 2001a, 'Is the resource-based "view" a useful perspective for strategic management research?', *Academy of Management Review*, vol. 26, no. 1, pp. 22–41.

Priem, R. and Butler, J. 2001b, 'Tautology in the resource-based view and the implications of externally determined resource values: Further comments', *Academy of Management Review*, vol. 26, no. 1, pp. 57–67.

Provan, K.G. and Skinner, S.J. 1989, 'Interorganizational dependence and control predictors of opportunism in dealer–supplier relations', *Academy of Management Journal*, vol. 32, no. 1, pp. 202–212.

Ratnasingam, P. 2004, 'The impact of collaborative commerce and trust in web services', *Journal of Enterprise Information Management*, vol. 17, no. 5, pp. 382–387.

Ray, G., Barney, J.B. and Muhanna, W.A. 2004, 'Capabilities, business processes, and competitive advantage: Choosing the dependent variable in empirical tests of the resource-based view', *Strategic Management Journal*, vol. 25, no. 1, pp. 23–37.

Rayport, J.F. and Sviokla, J.J. 1995, 'Exploiting the virtual value chain', *Harvard Business Review*, vol. 73, no. 6, pp. 75–85.

Reed, R. and DeFillippi, R. 1990, 'Causal ambiguity, barriers to imitation, and sustainable competitive advantage', *Academy of Management Review*, vol. 15, no. 1, pp. 88–102.

Reich, B.H. and Benbasat, I. 1996, 'Measuring the linkage between business and information technology objectives', *MIS Quarterly*, vol. 20, no. 1, pp. 55–81.

Richardson, G.B. 1972, 'The organization of industry', *Economic Journal*, vol. 82, no. 327, pp. 883–896.

Rindova, V. and Formbrun, C. 1999, 'Constructing competitive advantage: The role of firm-constituent interactions', *Strategic Management Journal*, vol. 20, no. 8, pp. 691–710.

Rindova, V. and Kotha, S. 2001, 'Continuous "morphing": Competing through dynamic capabilities form and function', *Academy of Management Journal*, vol. 44, no. 6, pp. 1263–1280.

Roberts, L., Brown, D. and Pirani, M. 1990, 'Information strategies: Motor dealerships and the Porter thesis', *Management Decision*, vol. 28, no. 7, pp. 22–25.

Robins, J. and Wiersma, M. 1995, 'A resource-based approach to the multibusiness firm: Empirical analysis of portfolio interrelationships and corporate financial performance', *Strategic Management Journal*, vol. 16, no. 4, pp. 277–299.

Robinson, K. 1998, 'An examination of the influence of industry structure on eight alternative measures of new venture performance for high potential independent new ventures', *Journal of Business Venturing*, vol. 14, no. 2, pp. 165–187.

Romer, P. 1990, 'Endogenous technological change', *Journal of Political Economy*, vol. 98, no. 5, pp. 71–102.

Rooney, P. 2002, *XML Web Services: Brand-New Key for SMBs*. Available: www.crn.com [2007, February].

Rosenberg, N. 2000, *Schumpeter and the Endogeneity of Technology: Some American perspectives*, Second edn, Routledge, London.

Rosenberg, N. 1982, *Inside the Black Box: Technology and Economics*, Cambridge University Press, New York.

Rosenberg, N. 1976, 'On technological expectations', *The Economic Journal*, vol. 86, no. 343, pp. 523–535.

Rosenbloom, R. 2000, 'Leadership, capabilities, and technological change: The transformation of NCR in the electronic era', *Strategic Management Journal*, vol. 21, no. 10/11, pp. 1083–1108.

Rosenkopf, L. and Nerkar, A. 2001, 'Beyond local search: Boundary spanning, exploitation, and impact in the optical disk industry', *Strategic Management Journal*, vol. 22, no. 4, pp. 287–306.

Ross, J., Beath, C. and Goodhoe, D. 1996, 'Develop long-term competitiveness through IT assets', *MIT Sloan Management Review*, vol. 38, no. 1, pp. 31–42.

Rossman, G.B. and Rallis, S.F. 1998, *Learning in the Field: An Introduction into Qualitative Research*, Sage, Thousand Oaks, CA.

Rostow, W.W. 1991, 'Foreword' in *Opening Doors: The Life and Work of Joseph Schumpeter*, ed. R.L. Allen, Transaction Publishers, New Jersey.

Rothaermel, F. 2001, 'Incumbent's advantage through exploiting complementary assets via interfirm cooperation', *Strategic Management Journal*, vol. 22, no. 6/7, pp. 687–699.

Rouse, M. and Daellenbach, U. 1999, 'Rethinking research methods for the resource-based perspective: Isolating sources of sustainable competitive advantage', *Strategic Management Journal*, vol. 20, no. 5, pp. 487–494.

Rubin, P.H. 1973, 'The expansion of firms', *Journal of Political Economy*, vol. 81, no. 4, pp. 936–949.

Ruiz-Mercader, J., Meroño-Cerdan, A.L. and Sabater-Sánchez, R. 2006, 'Information technology and learning: Their relationship and impact on organisational performance in small businesses', *International Journal of Information Management*, vol. 26, no. 1, pp. 16–29.

Rumelt, R.P. 1984, 'Towards a strategic theory of the firm' in *Competitive Strategic Management*, ed. R. Lamb, Englewood Cliffs, NJ, pp. 556–570.

Rumelt, R. and Wensley, R. 1981, 'In search of the market share effect' in *Academy of Management Proceedings*, ed. K. Chung, Academy of Management, San Diego, CA., pp. 2–6.

Russo, M.V. Fouts, P.A. 1997, 'A resource-based perspective on corporate environmental performance and profitability', *Academy of Management Journal*, vol. 40, no. 3, pp. 534–559.

Saban, K. and Rau, S. 2005, 'The functionality of websites as export marketing channels for small and medium enterprises', *Electronic Markets*, vol. 15, no. 2, pp. 128–135.

Sager, M. 1988, 'Competitive information systems in Australian retail banking', *Information and Management*, vol. 15, no. 1, pp. 59–67.

Salancik, G.R. 1982, 'Commitment and the control of organizational behavior and belief' in *New Dimensions in Organizational Behavior*, eds. B.M. Staw and G.R. Salancik, Robert E. Krieger, Malabar, FL. pp. 1–54.

Sambamurthy, V. and Zmud, R.W. 1992, *Managing IT for Success: The Empowering Business Partnership*, Financial Executives Research Foundation, Washington, DC.

Sandberg, W. and Hofer, C.W. 1987, 'Improving new venture performance: The role of strategy, industry structure, and the entrepreneur', *Journal of Business Venturing*, vol. 2, no. 1, pp. 475–535.

Santarelli, E. and Pesciarelli, E. 1990, 'The emergence of a vision: The development of Schumpeter's theory of entrepreneurship', *History of Political Economy*, vol. 22, pp. 677–696.

Santhanam, R. and Hartono, E. 2003, 'Issues in linking information technology capability to firm performance', *MIS Quarterly*, vol. 27, no. 1, pp. 125–153.

Schendel, D.E. and Patton, G.R. 1978, 'A simultaneous equation model of corporate strategy', *Management Science*, vol. 24, no. 15, pp. 1611–1621.

Schlemmer, F. and Webb, B. 2006, 'The impact of strategic assets on financial performance and on internet performance', *Electronic Markets*, vol. 16, no. 4, pp. 371–385.

Schlenker, L. and Crocker, N. 2003, 'Building an e-business scenario for small businesses: The IBM SME Gateway project', *Qualitative Market Research: An International Journal*, vol. 6, no. 1, pp. 7–17.

Schmid, B. 2001, 'What is new about the digital economy', *Electronic Markets*, vol. 11, no. 1, pp. 44–51.

Schoemaker, P.H. 1990, 'Strategy, complexity and economic rent', *Management Science*, vol. 36, no. 10, pp. 1178–1192.

Schroder, D. and Madeja, N. 2004, 'Is customer relationship management a success factor in electronic commerce?', *Journal of Electronic Commerce Research*, vol. 5, no. 1, pp. 38–52.

Schumpeter, J.A. 1911, *Theorie der wirtschaftlichen Entwicklung*, Dunker and Humbolt, Leipzig.

Schumpeter, J.A. 1928, 'The instability of capitalism', *Economic Journal*, vol. 38, pp. 361–386.

Schumpeter, J.A. 1934, *Theory of Economic Development*, Harvard University Press, Cambridge, MA.

Schumpeter, J.A. 1939, *Business Cycles*, McGraw-Hill, New York.

Schumpeter, J.A. 1942, *Capitalism, Socialism and Democracy*, Harper & Brothers, New York.

Schumpeter, J.A. 1943, *Capitalism, Socialism and Democracy*, Second edn, Allen and Unwin, London.

Schumpeter, J.A. 1947, *Capitalism, Socialism and Democracy*, second edn, George Allen and Unwin, London.

Schumpeter, J.A. 1951, 'Economic theory and entrepreneurial history' in *Essays of Economic Topics of J.A. Schumpeter*, ed. R.V. Clemence, Kennikat Press, Port Washington, pp. 248–266.

Schumpeter, J.A. 1955, *Theory of Economic Development*, Harvard University Press, Cambridge, MA.

Schumpeter, J.A. and Schumpeter, E.B. 1954, *History of Economic Analysis*, Oxford University Press New York.

Schwarzer, B. 1995, 'Organizing global IS management to meet competitive challenges: Experiences from the pharmaceutical industry', *Journal of Global Information Management*, vol. 3, no. 1, pp. 5–16.

Sher, P. and Lee, V. 2004, 'Information technology as a facilitator for enhancing dynamic capabilities through knowledge management', *Information and Management*, vol. 41, no. 8, pp. 933–945.

Shionoya, Y. 1996, 'The sociology of science and Schumpeter's ideology' in *Joseph A. Schumpeter, Historian of Economics*, ed. L.A. Moss, Routledge, London and New York.

Short, J. and Venkatraman, N. 1992, 'Beyond business process redesign: Redefining Baxter's business network', *Sloan Management Review*, vol. 34, no. 1, pp. 7–20.

Sicilia, M.A., Lytras, M., Rodriguez, E. and Garcia-Barriocanal, E. 2006, 'Integrating descriptions of knowledge management learning activities into large ontological structures: A case study', *Data and Knowledge Engineering*, vol. 57, no. 2, pp. 111–121.

Silverman, D. 1999, 'Qualitative research: Meanings or practices?', *Information Systems Journal*, vol. 8, no. 3, pp. 3–20.

Silverman, D. 1993, *Interpreting Qualitative Data*, Sage Publications, London.

Simon, H.A. 1955, 'A behavioral model of rational choice', *Quarterly Journal of Economics*, vol. 69, no. 1, pp. 99–118.

Singh, J., Tucker, D. and House, R. 1986, 'Organizational legitimacy and the liability of newness', *Administrative Science Quarterly*, vol. 31, no. 2, pp. 171–193.

Smith, H. and Fingar, P. 2003, *Business Process Management: The Third Wave*, Meghan-Kiffer Press, Florida, US.

Smith, K.G., Ferrier, W.J. and Ndofor, H. 2001, 'Competitive Dynamics Research: Critique and Future Directions' in *Handbook of Strategic Managment*, ed. M.A. Hitt, R.E. Freeman and Jeffrey S. Harrison, Blackwell Publishers, Oxford, pp. 315–361.

Song, M., Droge, C., Hanvanich, S. and Calantone, R. 2005, 'Marketing and technology resource complementarity: An analysis of their interaction effect in two environmental contexts', *Strategic Management Journal*, vol. 26, no. 3, pp. 259–276.

Sorenson, J.B. and Stuart, T.E. 2000, 'Aging, obsolescence and organizational innovation', *Administrative Science Quarterly*, vol. 45, no. 4, pp. 81–112.

Stal, M. 2002, 'Web services beyond component-based computing', *Communications of the ACM*, vol. 45, no. 10, pp. 71–76.

Staw, B. 1997, 'The escalation of commitment: An update and appraisal' in *Organizational Decision Making*, ed. Z. Shapira, Cambridge University Press, New York, pp. 191–215.

Straub, D. and Watson, R. 2001, 'Research commentary: Transformational issues in researching IS and net-enabled organisations', *Information Systems Research*, vol. 12, no. 4, pp. 335–345.

Strauss, A.L. and Corbin, J. 1990, *Basics of Qualitative Research: Grounded Theory Procedures and Techniques*, Sage, Newbury Park, CA.

Stuart, T. 2000, 'Inter-organizational alliances and the performance of firms: A study of growth and innovation rates in a high-technology industry', *Strategic Management Journal*, vol. 21, no. 8, pp. 791–811.

Sull, D.N. 1999, 'Why good companies go bad', *Harvard Business Review*, vol. 77, no. 4, pp. 42–52.

Sward, D.S. 2006, *Measuring the Business Value of Information Technology: Practical Strategies for IT and Business Managers*, Intel Press, Hillsboro, OR.

Swedberg, R. 1991, *Joseph A. Schumpeter*, Polity Press, Cambridge, UK.

Tavakolian, H. 1989, 'Linking the information technology structure with organizational competitive advantage: A survey', *MIS Quarterly*, vol. 13, no. 3, pp. 309–317.

Teece, D.J. 1980, 'Economies of scope and the scope of the enterprise.', *Journal of Economic Behaviour & Organization*, vol. 1, pp. 223–247.

Teece, D. 1986, 'Profiting from technological innovation: Implications for integration, collaboration, licensing and public policy', *Research Policy*, vol. 15, no. 6, pp. 285–305.

Teece, D. 1992, 'Competition, cooperation, and innovation: Organizational arrangements for regimes of rapid technological progress', *Journal of Economic Behavior & Organization*, vol. 18, no. 1, pp. 1–25.

Teece, D.J., Pisano, G. and Shuen, A. 1997, 'Dynamic capabilities and strategic management', *Strategic Management Journal*, vol. 18, no. 7, pp. 509–533.

Teece, D.J., Dosi, G., Rumelt, R. and Winter, S.G. 1994, 'Understanding corporate coherence: Theory and evidence', *Journal of Economic Behaviour and Organization*, vol. 23, pp. 1–30.

Teo, T.H. and Choo, W. 2001, 'Assessing the impact of using the internet for competitive intelligence', *Information and Management*, vol. 39, no. 1, pp. 67–83.

Theodorou, P. and Florou, G. 2006, 'Manufacturing strategies and financial performance: The effect of advanced information technology: CAD/CAM systems', *Omega*, vol. 36, no. 1, pp. 107–121.

Thong, J.L. 2001, 'Resource constraints and information systems implementation in Singaporean small businesses', *Omega*, vol. 29, no. 2, pp. 143–156.

Tigre, P. and Dedrick, J. 2004, 'E-commerce in Brazil: Local adoption of a global technology', *Electronic Markets*, vol. 14, no. 1, pp. 36–48.

Tippins, M. and Sohi, R. 2003, 'IT competency and firm performance: Is organizational learning the missing link?', *Strategic Management Journal*, vol. 24, no. 8, pp. 745–761.

Tosi, H. and Slocum, J. 1984, 'Contingency theory: Some directions', *Journal of Management*, vol. 10, no. 1, pp. 9–26.

Tripsas, M. and Gavetti, G. 2000, 'Capabilities, cognition, and inertia: Evidence from digital imaging', *Strategic Management Journal*, vol. 21, no. 10/11, pp. 1147–1161.

Tyran, C., Dennis, A., Vogel, D. and Nunamaker, J. 1992, 'The application of electronic meeting technology to support strategic management', *MIS Quarterly*, vol. 16, no. 3, pp. 313–334.

Ulfelder, S. 2003, 'GM gears up with collaboration based on web services', *Network World*, May, pp. 26–63.

Vancil, R.F. 1972, 'Better management for corporate development', *Harvard Business Review*, vol. 50, no. 5, pp. 53–62.

Venkatraman, N. and Ramanujam, V. 1986, 'Measurement of business performance in strategy research: A comparison of approaches', *Academy of Management Review*, vol. 11, no. 4, pp. 801–814.

Venkatraman, N. and Ramanujam, V. 1987, 'Measurement of business economic performance: An examination of method convergence', *Journal of Management*, vol. 13, no. 1, pp. 109–122.

Venkatraman, N. and Zaheer, A. 1990, 'Electronic integration and strategic advantage: Quasi-experimental study in the insurance industry', *Information Systems Research*, vol. 1, no. 4, pp. 377–393.

Verhees, F.H.M. and Meulenberg, M.G. 2004, 'Market orientation, innovativeness, product innovation, and performance in small firms', *Journal of Small Business Management*, vol. 42, no. 2, pp. 134–154.

Verona, G. and Ravasi, D. 2003, 'Unbundling dynamic capabilities: An exploratory study of continuous product innovation', *Industrial and Corporate Change*, vol. 12, no. 3, pp. 577–606.

Wade, M. and Hulland, J. 2004, 'The resource-based view and information systems research: Review, extension, and suggestions for future research', *MIS Quarterly*, vol. 28, no. 1, pp. 107–142.

Walton, R. 1989, *Up and Running: Integrating Information Technology and the Organization*, Harvard Business School Press, Cambridge, MA.

Warner, T.N. 1987, 'Information technology as a competitive burden', *Sloan Management Review*, vol. 29, no. 1, pp. 55–61.

Warriner, D. 1931, 'Schumpeter and the conception of static equilibrium', *The Economic Journal*, vol. 41, no. 161, pp. 38–50.

Webb, B. and Sayer, R. 1998, 'Benchmarking small companies on the internet', *Long Range Planning*, vol. 19, no. 6, pp. 815–827.

Webb, B. and Schlemmer, F. 2006, 'Resilience as a source of competitive advantage for small information technology companies' in *The Transfer and Diffusion of Information Technology for Organizational Resilience*, eds. B. Donnellan, T.J. Larsen, L. Levine and J.I. DeGross, Springer, New York, pp. 181–198.

Webb, B. and Schlemmer, F. 2008, 'Predicting web services performance from internet performance: An empirical study of resources and capabilities in e-business SMEs', *Journal of Knowledge Management*, vol. 12, no. 6 (forthcoming).

Weick, K.E. 1979, *The Social Psychology of Organizing*, 2nd edn, Addison-Wesley, Reading, MA.

Welsh, J. and White, J. 1981, 'A small business is not a little big business', *Harvard Business Review*, vol. 59, no. 4, pp. 18–32.

Wernerfelt, B. 1984, 'A resource-based view of the firm', *Strategic Management Journal*, vol. 5, no. 2, pp. 171–180.

Wetlaufer, S. 2000, 'Common sense and conflict: An interview with Disney's Michael Eisner', *Harvard Business Review*, vol. 78, no. 1, pp. 114–124.

Whitley, R. 1992, *The Customer Driven Company*, Addison-Wesley, Reading, MA.

Wiley, N. 1988, 'The micro–macro problem in social theory', *Sociological Theory*, vol. 6, pp. 254–261.

Willcocks, L. and Lester, S. 1996, 'Beyond the IT productivity paradox', *European Management Journal*, vol. 14, no. 3, pp. 279–290.

Williamson, O.E. 1991, 'Strategizing, economizing, and economic organization', *Strategic Management Journal*, vol. 12, pp. 75–94.

Winter, S. 1987, 'Knowledge and competence as strategic assets' in *The Competitive Challenge*, ed. D. Teece, Center for Research in Management, Berkeley, CA, pp. 159–184.

Winter, S. 2003, 'Understanding dynamic capabilities', *Strategic Management Journal*, vol. 24, no. 10, pp. 991–995.

Winter, S.G. 2006, 'Toward a neo-Schumpeterian theory of the firm', *Industrial and Corporate Change*, vol. 15, no. 1, pp. 125–141.

Woo, C.Y. 1987, 'Path analysis of the relationship between market share, business-level conduct and risk', *Strategic Management Journal*, vol. 8, no. 2, pp. 149–168.

Woo, C.Y. and Cooper, A.C. 1981, 'Strategies of effective low share businesses', *Strategic Management Journal*, vol. 2, no. 3, pp. 301–318.

Yeoh, P. and Roth, K. 1999, 'An empirical analysis of sustained advantage in the U.S. pharmaceutical industry: Impact of firm resources and capabilities', *Strategic Management Journal*, vol. 20, no. 7, pp. 637–653.

Yoo, S. and Choi, H.J. 1990, 'Managing on a computer at a Korean insurance company', *Long Range Planning*, vol. 23, no. 1, pp. 69–78.

Young, G., Smith, K. G. and Grimm, C. 1996, 'Austrian and industrial organization perspectives on firm-level competitive activity and performance', *Organization Science*, vol. 73, pp. 243–254.

Zahra, S. and Nielsen, A. 2002, 'Sources of capabilities, integration and technology commercialization', *Strategic Management Journal*, vol. 23, no. 5, pp. 377–398.

Zhang, M. and Lado, A. 2001, 'Information Systems and competitive advantage: A competency-based view', *Technovation*, vol. 21, no. 3, pp. 147–156.

Zhu, K. 2004, 'The complementarity of information technology infrastructure and e-commerce capability: A resource-based assessment of their business value', *Journal of Management Information Systems*, vol. 21, no. 1, pp. 167–202.

Zhu, K. and Kraemer, K. 2002, 'e-commerce metrics for Net-enhanced organizations: Assessing the value of e-commerce to firm-performance in the manufacturing sector', *Information Systems Research*, vol. 13, no. 3, pp. 275–295.

Zhu, K., Kraemer, K. and Xu, S. 2002, 'A cross-country study of electronic business adoption using the technology–organization–environment framework', *Twenty-Third International Conference on Information Systems*, pp. 337–351.

Zhuang, Y. and Lederer, A. 2006, 'A resource-based view of electronic commerce', *Information and Management*, vol. 43, no. 2, pp. 251–261.

Zollo, M. and Winter, S. 2002, 'Deliberate learning and the evolution of dynamic capabilities', *Organization Science*, vol. 13, no. 3, pp. 339–351.

Index

For Product Safety Concerns and Information please contact our
EU representative GPSR@taylorandfrancis.com Taylor & Francis
Verlag GmbH, Kaufingerstraße 24, 80331 München, Germany